MEYDAN SHOPPING SQUARE

jovis

MEYDAN SHOPPING SQUARE

EIN NEUER PROTOTYP VON FOA
A NEW PROTOTYPE BY FOA

A METRO Group Project in Istanbul

Mit Fotografien von With Photographs by
Murat Pulat

Cornelia Tomerius

Herausgegeben von Edited by
Michael Cesarz
Manina Ferreira-Erlenbach

jovis

INHALT CONTENT

Welcher Bauherr träumt nicht davon, ein maßgebliches Gebäude zu schaffen – einen Ort, über den die Menschen reden und an den sie gerne zurückkehren?

Wir wollten es wagen, Seh- und Einkaufsgewohnheiten zu brechen, um Maßstäblichkeit in den Handel zurück zu bringen. So entstand die Idee zu Meydan, dem ersten Shopping Square der Welt. „Meydan" heißt aus dem Türkischen übersetzt so viel wie „Platz". Unser Shopping Square ist ein moderner Marktplatz, der zum neuen Zentrum des Istanbuler Stadtteils Ümraniye avanciert. Kein hohles Gefäß, sondern ein lebendiger Teil der Stadt, der einer wuchernden Urbanität helfen wird, eine eigene Identität zu entwickeln. Nicht „auf", sondern „unter" einer grünen Wiese entstand dieser Solitär. Gefaltete, begehbare, grüne Dächer mit Zuwegungen aus allen Himmelsrichtungen entwickeln ihre Faszination in einer von Beton dominierten Großstadtwelt. Ein großer offener Platz gründet die Mitte einer luftigen Einkaufswelt, die in Themen gegliedert wurde wie die alten Basargassen am Bosporus. Nicht zuletzt haben wir einen Bau von nachhaltiger Wirkung geschaffen. Eine der größten Geothermie-Anlagen Europas klimatisiert das Gebäude sommers wie winters.

Meydan trägt die Handschrift der Londoner Foreign Office Architects (FOA), die mit diesem Projekt erstmals auch in der Handelsarchitektur Signale setzen. 2005 hatten sie sich in einem von der METRO Group Asset Management ausgerichteten Workshop mit fünf international renommierten Architekten-Teams durchgesetzt, indem sie die Spur historischer Stadtkerne aufgenommen und daraus ein Center des dritten Jahrtausends entwickelt haben. Eine der größten Herausforderungen des Entwurfs war die Dachkonstruktion. Falten und Einschnitte bilden das Prinzip der Dachlandschaft: Der Boden wird zur Wand, Treppen und Rampen verschmelzen in der Oberfläche. Faltungen verkleinern die Maßstäbe, erzeugen Nähe. Enorme Spannweiten von 16 Metern wurden durch das Prinzip der Kuppelform möglich. Die Anwendung des Structural-Glazing-Prinzips vermindert die Trennung zwischen Läden und Platz auf eine zwei Zentimeter dünne Glashaut. Somit wird das Handelsgeschehen transparent und weckt die Neugier. Der Kaufakt selbst ist erlebbar wie auf einem offenen Markt. Das Herzstück des gesamten Komplexes, der Platz, wurde in Anlehnung an die rötliche Erde in 700 000 terrakottafarbenen Lehmziegeln ausgeführt. Er bietet letztlich den Raum zum Leben, der den Shopping Square aus der Masse der glitzernden Konsumtempel heraushebt. Hier mag man sitzen, reden, spielen, ausruhen, lesen, arbeiten, träumen und schauen.

Auch das 30 000 Quadratmeter große Gründach bietet Platz zum Verweilen, erfüllt aber zugleich wichtige Funktionen für das Gebäudeklima: Es hält den Regen zurück, bindet Staub- und Luftschadstoffe und schirmt Hitze wie Kälte ab.

Inspiriert von der islamischen Architektur wurden viele der Außenfassaden perforiert. Durch den Wechsel von verschiedenen Raumtiefen hinter einer Terrakottahaut wird die Massivität der Körper zusätzlich aufgeweicht. Dieser Effekt wird am Abend besonders deutlich, wenn die Baukörper von innen heraus beleuchtet werden. In Meydan strahlt die Architektur selbst.

VORWORT
FOREWORD

What property developer does not dream of creating a significant building – a place that people talk about, and to which they want to return?

We wanted to have the courage to break looking and shopping habits, in order to bring significance back into commerce. This is how the idea for Meydan, the world's first shopping square, came into being. The word 'Meydan' in Turkish means 'square'. Our shopping square is a modern market place, which has developed into the new centre of the Ümraniye district of Istanbul. Not a hollow container, but a living part of the city, which will help a proliferating urban life to develop its own identity. This solitaire building was created not on, but below a green meadow. Folded, accessible, green roofs, with routes leading to them from all directions, exert their fascination in a concrete-dominated metropolitan world. A large open square forms the centre of an airy shopping world, which is divided into thematic areas like the old bazaar streets by the Bosphorus. Not least, we have created a building of lasting influence. The structure's climate is regulated, summer and winter, by one of Europe's largest geothermal systems.

Meydan bears the handwriting of the London firm Foreign Office Architects (FOA), who are setting another new direction with this project, their first in commercial architecture. In 2005 they asserted themselves in a workshop organized by the METRO Group Asset Management for five internationally renowned architectural teams, by picking up the traces of historic city centres and developing from them a centre for the new millennium. One of the greatest challenges for their design was the roof construction. Folds and incisions characterize the principle of a roof landscape. A ceiling becomes a wall, steps and ramps merge into the surface. Folding decreases the scale, and creates proximity. Enormous spans of 16 metres were made possible by the use of the dome form. The application of the structural glazing principle reduces the separation between shops and square to a glass skin of two centimetres in thickness. This makes the shopping event transparent and arouses curiosity. The act of purchasing itself can be experienced as though in an open market. The heart of the overall complex, the square, was carried out in 700,000 terracotta-coloured clay tiles in allusion to the local reddish soil. Finally, it offers the space to live that lifts the shopping square out of the mass of glittering temples of shopping. Here the shopper can sit, talk, play, rest, read, work, dream and observe.

The green roof, 30,000 square metres in area, also offers space to linger, but at the same time also fulfils important functions for the climate of the building: it keeps off the rain, filters out dust and pollution, and protects from both heat and cold.

Inspired by Islamic architecture, many of the exterior façades have been perforated. Through the alternation of various spatial depth behind a terracotta skin, the massivity of the buildings has additionally been softened. This effect becomes particularly noticeable in the evening, when the buildings are lit from within. In Meydan, the architecture itself shines.

Meydan bietet nicht nur reichlich Auswahl in 50 Geschäften. Für Unterhaltung und Entspannung sorgen ein Kinopalast, zahlreiche Restaurants und Cafés. Handel ist heute Teil der Unterhaltung. Beides muss einhergehen, um Zugkraft zu entfalten. Zugpferde des Handelns in Meydan sind Real, der erste Media Markt auf türkischem Boden und Ikea, das bereits 2005 auf diesem 130 000 Quadratmeter großen Terrain angesiedelt worden war. Gap, Mango, Nike, Adidas – Marken für junge Menschen. Tausende sind bereits Fan des Shopping Square, der nicht nur für Istanbul einmalig ist.
Die Verführung der Architektur geht einher mit Nachhaltigkeit und Verantwortung für künftige Generationen. Das neue Zentrum von Ümraniye ist eine Oase innovativer, umweltverträglicher Technologie. Um die Erdwärme zu nutzen, wurden mehr als 200 Erdwärmesonden in den Boden eingelassen. Insgesamt mehr als 18 Kilometer lange Leitungen sorgen für den Wärmeaustausch. Im Sommer machen wir uns die Erdkühle zu nutze, im Winter die Erdwärme. Dadurch arbeitet die Technik wesentlich effizienter als herkömmliche Systeme. Die Anlage spart jährlich 1,3 Millionen Kilowattstunden Primärenergie ein. Für die Anlage in Ümraniye wurde eine CO_2-Einsparung von 350 Tonnen pro Jahr berechnet.
Gewohnheiten verändern, das Handeln wieder sichtbar machen. Gelände und Gebäude an den Lebensgewohnheiten ausrichten und den Ort der Handlung zum Leben erwecken. Die Natur und somit das Leben schützen. Das sind die Maßstäbe in Meydan. Viel Freude bei der Lektüre und an der Entdeckung einer neuen Dimension: des ersten Shopping Squares der Welt.

Prof. Michael Cesarz ist CEO der METRO Group Asset Management, der Immobiliengesellschaft der METRO Group, einem der größten Handelsunternehmen der Welt. Der Shopping Square Meydan ist weltweit das größte Center des Konzerns.

Meydan offers a more than generous choice in 50 shops. Entertainment and relaxation are provided by a cinema, restaurants and cafés. Shopping today is part of the entertainment. Both must go together in order to enhance appeal. The drawing cards of shopping in Meydan are Real, the first media market on Turkish soil, and Ikea, which had already been established on this 130,000-square-metre terrain as early as 2005. Gap, Mango, Nike, Adidas – brand names for young people. Thousands are already fans of the shopping square, which is unique, and not only in Istanbul.

The seductiveness of the architecture goes along with sustainability and responsibility for future generations. The new centre of Ümraniye is an oasis of innovative, environmentally friendly technology. In order to make use of terrestrial heat, more than 200 geothermal probes were sunk into the soil. Pipes totalling more than 18 kilometres in length provide heat exchange. In both summer and winter, the temperatures of the earth are put to use. As a result, the technology works substantially more efficiently than traditional systems. The complex saves 1.3 million kilowatt-hours of primary energy annually. For the Ümraniye project, an annual saving of 350 tonnes of carbon dioxide was calculated.

Changing habits, making shopping visible again, organizing the area and the buildings according to life habits, and awakening the site to life; protecting nature and thus protecting life – these are the standards of Meydan. Enjoy reading about it and discovering a new dimension: the world's first shopping square.

Prof. Michael Cesarz is CEO of METRO Group Asset Management, the property branch of the METRO Group, one of the largest commercial enterprises in the world. The Shopping Square Meydan is the company's largest centre worldwide.

Wenn es Tag wird in Istanbul und der Muezzin seinen ersten Gebetsgesang anstimmt; und die Fischer auf dem Bosporus ihre Angeln auswerfen, während über ihnen, auf den beiden einzigen Brücken, welche die Kontinente verbinden, die Autos zum ersten Mal an diesem Tag im Stau stecken bleiben; und aus den Szene-Clubs im historischen Zentrum die letzten Nachtschwärmer auf die Straße treten, während anderswo schon die Angestellten in die gläsernen Bürotürme hasten; dann, wenn es Tag wird in Istanbul, ist die Stadt über Nacht mal wieder um fast tausend Bewohner gewachsen.

Istanbul wächst nach Sonnenuntergang. Dann wird in den Randbezirken der Stadt gehämmert und gesägt. Bis zum Morgen müssen die Siedler aus der Provinz ihre Häuschen fertig haben, Bretterbuden mit Blechdach und Fenster, die aufgrund der freiwilligen Nachtschicht „Gecekondu" – über Nacht gebaut – genannt werden. Der Grund zur Eile: Nach einem alten osmanischen Grundsatz darf jeder, der es schafft, in einer Nacht eine Behausung mit Dach zu errichten, den Grund und Boden darunter behalten. Bis heute wird die Landnahme nach dem Selbstbedienungsprinzip vielerorts geduldet. Und so wächst die Stadt ohne Kontrolle – und in einem enormen Tempo. In den 1950er Jahren zählte Istanbul gerade mal eine Million Einwohner, heute sind es zwölfmal, wenn nicht gar fast zwanzigmal so viel. „Zur Stadt", so kann man Istanbuls Namen übersetzen: Als die Osmanen sich im 14. Jahrhundert Konstantinopel näherten, stießen sie auf griechische Wegweiser, die sie als Ortseingangsschild missdeuteten. Heute wüsste man kaum, wo man solche Hinweisschilder – „Zur Stadt" – aufstellen sollte. Die Stadt ist überall.

Während Istanbul an seinen Enden immer weiter ausfranst, verdichtet es sich in seinem Inneren. Eine Hochhaussiedlung nach der anderen wächst gen Himmel – vor allem auf der asiatischen Seite Istanbuls, wo seit langem vorwiegend gewohnt wird, während man auf der anderen Seite des Bosporus, der europäischen, arbeitet. Oft sind es „Gated Communities", die hier entstehen, kleine nach außen geschlossene Mini-Städte mitten in der Stadt: Wohnsiedlungen mit eigenen Straßen und Schulen, Geschäften und Grünanlagen. Und auch die Gecekondus gehen nicht nur in die Breite. Wenn die Regierung mal wieder eine Amnestie erlässt und die nun legalen Grundbesitzer ein Stockwerk nach dem nächsten aufbauen, wachsen sie auch – wie die schicken Wohnsiedlungen für die Besserverdienenden – in die Höhe.

Doch beim Wachsen und Verdichten wird eines oft übersehen: An allen Ecken und Enden fehlt es der Metropole an Oasen der Ruhe, an öffentlichen Plätzen, auf denen Menschen zusammenkommen, Kultur erleben und Entspannung finden. Orte also, an denen Gemeinschaft stattfindet, Durchmischung möglich ist und die Stadt „durchatmen" kann. „Für Urbanität sind unkontrollierte Räume essenziell wichtig, in denen sich Öffentlichkeit herstellen kann", so der Berliner Stadtsoziologe Hartmut Häußermann. „Third Places" nennt der amerikanische Soziologe Ray Oldenburg in seinem Buch *The Great Good Place* die sozialen Räume, an denen – neben dem Arbeitsplatz und der Wohnung – Kommunikation und Interaktion im Vordergrund stehen, Zentren des menschlichen Zusammenlebens also. Und die amerikanische Stadtplanungsforscherin Toni Sachs-Pfeiffer fand heraus, dass Menschen ein tiefes Bedürfnis nach Plätzen haben, auf denen sie in

EINE MITTE FÜR ÜMRANIYE
A CENTRE FOR ÜMRANIYE

When day breaks in Istanbul and the muezzin begins to intone his first prayer, and the fishermen on the Bosphorus throw out their lines, while above them, on the only two bridges that link the continents, the cars come to a halt in the first traffic jam of the day; and the last nocturnal revellers emerge onto the street from the trendy clubs in the historic centre, while elsewhere employees are already hastening to work in the glass office towers; then, when day is breaking in Istanbul, the city has once again grown overnight by nearly a thousand inhabitants.

Istanbul grows after sunset. Then there is hammering and sawing in the suburbs on the edges of the city. The settlers from the country must have their little dwelling ready by morning, wooden booths with sheet-metal roofs and windows, called gecekondu – built overnight – on account of this voluntary night shift. The reason for this haste? According to an old Ottoman tradition, anyone who manages to build a dwelling-place with a roof in one night is entitled to the land on which he builds. Up to the present day, this commandeering of land on the self-service principle is tolerated in many places. And thus the city grows unchecked – and at a frantic speed. In the 1950s Istanbul had barely a million inhabitants; today there are twelve times, if not quite twenty times that figure. Istanbul's name means 'to the city' – when the Ottomans reached Constantinople in the fourteenth century, they encountered Greek road signs which they misinterpreted as signs pointing to the entrance of the city. Today one would hardly know where such signs reading 'To the city' should be placed. The city is everywhere.

While Istanbul continually branches out at its edges, in its centre it becomes denser. One high-rise residential building after another grows towards the sky – above all on Istanbul's Asian side, for a long time a predominantly residential area, while people go to work on the other side of the Bosphorus, the European side. Often it is 'gated communities' that come into being here, mini-cities closed to outsiders in the middle of the city: housing estates with their own streets and schools, shops and parks. And the gecekondus too grow, not only in breadth. The next time that the government declares another amnesty and the now legal landowners build up one storey after another, they too, like the fashionable housing enclaves for prosporous families, grow higher and higher into the sky.

But one thing is often overlooked in all this growth and agglomeration. What is everywhere missing from the metropolis is oases of peace, public places where people come together to experience culture and find opportunities to relax. Places, that is, where a community can develop, people can mingle and the city can breathe freely. 'For urban areas, the development of unsupervised public spaces is an essential necessity,' according to the Berlin urban sociologist Hartmut Häußermann. 'Third Places' is the caption given by the American sociologist Ray Oldenburg in his book *The Great Good Place* to the social spaces where – apart from the workplace and the home – communication and interaction are placed in the foreground, in other words, centres of human coexistence. And the American urban planning researcher Toni Sachs-Pfeiffer dis-

Ruhe sitzen oder für eine Weile stehen bleiben können, ohne einander im Weg zu sein. Die Marktplätze und Parkanlagen in den über Jahrhunderte gewachsenen Städten Europas erfüllen dieses Bedürfnis. Doch wohin sollen die Menschen in den rasant ausufernden Megacitys gehen, wo es vielleicht noch ein Zentrum gibt, aber drum herum inzwischen so viel Peripherie, dass sich der Weg dorthin für die meisten nicht lohnt?

Das Problem ist so alt wie das Wachstum der Städte. „Urban Sprawl" nennt man die Explosion der Städte, die Anfang des letzten Jahrhunderts vielerorts in Amerika zu beobachten war. Wer es sich leisten konnte, verließ die Stadt und zog in die Vororte. Neue Straßen, zunehmende Modernisierung und die staatliche Subventionierung des Eigenheimbaus machten den Umzug schließlich so attraktiv, dass ihn immer mehr Menschen auf sich nahmen. Die „klassischen" Wohnsuburbs entstanden: kleine Siedlungen, oft ohne eigene Infrastruktur, ohne Zentrum, ohne Charme.

So musste es zumindest Victor Gruen empfunden haben. Als der Architekt und Stadtplaner nach seiner Emigration aus Österreich Anfang der 1940er Jahre durch die amerikanischen Vororte spazierte, vermisste er einiges: Straßenzüge zum Promenieren, die gemütlichen Kaffeehäuser Wiens und nicht zuletzt die Passagen, die sich seit dem späten 19. Jahrhundert in Europa ausgebreitet hatten – überdachte Einkaufsstraßen, in denen das aufstrebende Bürgertum das bis dato auf schiere Beschaffung angelegte Einkaufen nun als beliebte Freizeitbeschäftigung zelebrierte. Außerdem störte den Architekten der zunehmende Verkehr. Am liebsten hätte Gruen, der übrigens unter dem Namen Victor David Grünbaum in Wien geboren wurde, wie aus seiner Heimatstadt gewohnt, sämtliche Besorgungen zu Fuß erledigt.

Ein wenig Europa, so befand Gruen nach den ersten Erfahrungen in seiner neuen Heimat, könne den Amerikanern nur gut tun: Also plante er in den zersiedelten Außenbezirken amerikanischer Großstädte den Bau eines modernen Marktplatzes, auf dem Menschen flanieren, einkaufen und Freizeit verbringen können; und damit kein schlechtes Wetter das Vergnügen stört, alles geschützt unter einem Dach, ähnlich wie bei den Passagen – das Shoppingcenter war erfunden. Doch Gruen dachte an mehr als den Kommerz: Schulen, Parks und Wohnhäuser wünschte er sich um seine Neuschöpfung – und die Mall als neue Mitte. Aus dem unüberschaubaren Vorortbrei sollte sich eine Vielzahl kleiner Städte entwickeln, mit eigenem Zentrum und von sozialer Lebendigkeit.

1956 wird Gruens erste überdachte „Shopping Mall" in Southdale, südlich von Minneapolis, gebaut. Neben Shops und Snacks finden die Besucher hier auch eine Schule, einen Hörsaal und einen Eislaufplatz. Drei Jahre später dann wurden in dem Städtchen Kalamazoo zwei Straßenblocks der Hauptstraße Burdick Street für den Autoverkehr gesperrt, um den Platz für eine Mall im Stadtzentrum zu räumen. Denn nicht nur im Vorort funktioniert Gruens Prinzip. Wo es keine gewachsene historische Altstadt gibt, die zum Verweilen einlädt, was in amerikanischen Städten nicht selten der Fall ist, wird das Shoppingcenter zum City Center.

covered that people have a deep need for places where they can sit or stand for a while in peace without getting in each other's way. The market places and car parks in the European cities that have grown up over the centuries fulfil this need. But where are people to go in the frantically expanding megacities, where there is perhaps still a centre, but round about it so much periphery that for most people it is not worth making the journey to it?

The problem is as old as the growth of cities. 'Urban sprawl' is the name given to the explosion of the cities that could be observed in many parts of America at the beginning of the last century. Everyone who could afford it left the city and moved into the suburbs. New roads, increasing modernization and state subsidies for own-home building finally made the move out of the city so attractive that increasingly people undertook it. The 'classical' residential suburbs came into being: small settlements, often without an infrastructure of their own, without a centre, without charm.

At any rate, that must be how Victor Gruen saw it. When this architect and urban planner took his walks through the American suburbs after his emigration from Austria in the early 1940s, there were some things he missed: streets for strolling along, the cosy coffee houses of Vienna, and not least the arcades that had spread throughout Europe since the late nineteenth century – roofed shopping streets, in which the rising bourgeoisie, until then intent on shopping merely for the sake of acquisition, now celebrated it as a favourite leisure activity. Another thing that disturbed Gruen – incidentally born in Vienna under the name Victor David Grünbaum – was the traffic. He would have preferred to carry out all his errands on foot, as he had been used to do in his native city.

A little touch of Europe, Gruen decided after his first experiences in his new home, could only be good for Americans. Thus, in the overdeveloped outer districts of American cities, he planned to build modern market places, where people could stroll, shop and spend their leisure time; and so that bad weather should not spoil their enjoyment, everything would be sheltered under one roof, just as with the arcades. The shopping centre had been invented. But Gruen had more than business interests in mind: he wanted his new creation to be surrounded by schools, parks and dwelling houses – with the mall as the new centre. From the huge confused mass of the suburbs, a multitude of small towns were to develop, with their own centres and their own lively social life.

In 1956 Gruen's first covered shopping mall was built in Southdale, south of Minneapolis. Here, apart from shops and snacks, visitors also found a school, a lecture theatre and an ice rink. Three years later in the little town of Kalamazoo two blocks in the main street, Burdick Street, were closed to traffic in order to clear space for a mall in the town centre. For it was not only in the suburbs that Gruen's principle worked. Where there is no original historic old city inviting the visitor to linger, which is not seldom the case in American cities, the shopping centre becomes the city centre.

Gruens Mall wurde ein Erfolg und das Prinzip mehrfach kopiert. Heute wird schon mal behauptet, Amerika habe mehr Shoppingcenter als Schulen. Und auch in Europa feierte die Mall Erfolge. Allerdings hatten die meisten von Gruens Nachahmern vorwiegend den geschäftlichen Erfolg im Blick – und weniger den städteplanerischen Impuls, der Gruen einst trieb. Und so wurden viele Shoppingcenter das, was der Österreicher vermeiden wollte, nämlich unifunktionale Zentren, in denen neben dem Einkaufserlebnis allenfalls ein wenig Gastronomie und Unterhaltung geboten werden, diese aber einzig und allein den Zweck verfolgen, die Menschen zum Kaufen zu animieren. Soziale und integrierende Funktionen haben diese Center, die oft ohne großen architektonischen Anspruch einige Geschäfte unter einem Dach vereinen, nicht mehr – und wenn doch, dann nur als willkommener Nebeneffekt. So blieb von Gruens Idee oft nur das übrig, was Rem Koolhaas später „Junk Space" nennen sollte – lieblos zusammengestückelte Konstruktionen mit künstlichem Licht, die sich als fensterlose Bauten mit ihren Rolltreppen unaufhaltsam in die Tiefe des Raumes vorarbeiten. Und Shopping, so Koolhaas, sei „die einzige Form öffentlichen Lebens, die uns geblieben ist". Doch zurück zu Istanbul. Genauer: nach Ümraniye. Die Geschichte dieses Stadtteils auf der asiatischen Seite ist symptomatisch für Istanbuls Wachstumsschub im letzten Jahrhundert. Bis 1950 war Ümraniye noch ein kleines Dorf am Stadtrand, das die Istanbuler allenfalls kannten, weil sie auf ihrem Ausflug an den Ferienort Sile am Schwarzen Meer mitten hindurch mussten. Der Bebauungsplan von 1980 hatte mit Ümraniye nichts Großes vor, vielmehr sollten die Ufer des Marmarameeres – von Kadıköy über Bostancı nach Maltepe und Kartal – entwickelt werden. Ümraniye erschien den Stadtplanern wenig attraktiv, versprach es doch weder unverbauten Meerblick noch die Nähe zum historischen Zentrum auf der europäischen Seite und stattdessen nur unwirtliches Gelände in Höhenlage. Was sie dabei jedoch nicht beachtet hatten: Ümraniye liegt genau zwischen den Zufahrtsstraßen zu den beiden Bosporusbrücken – die eine wurde 1973, die andere 1988 eingeweiht – und damit zwischen den lebenswichtigen Arterien der Stadt. Diese Lage machte den Landstrich schließlich attraktiv für Fabriken wie Firmensitze, für Wohnbauten wie Einkaufstempel. Heute haben etwa Bosch, Bayer und Siemens hier ihre Headquarters. In Ümraniye wohnen in etwa so viele Menschen wie in Düsseldorf und bis heute gehört der Stadtteil zu den am schnellsten wachsenden Quartieren Istanbuls – die Probleme, welche die rasante Ausdehnung mit sich bringt, wurden schon genannt: Auch hier fehlt es der Peripherie an einem Zentrum, an sozialen Plätzen für Gemeinschaft.

Eine Antwort auf dieses Problem versucht nun die METRO Group Asset Management. Und was sie hier, mitten in Ümraniye zwischen einem Autobahndreieck und aufschießenden Wohnbauten, plant, erinnert an die Visionen des Victor Gruen. Ein Shoppingcenter entsteht hier, das weit mehr sein will als der Versorger für die umliegenden Wohnblöcke. Hier soll ein Platz entstehen, eine Art Piazza, von Bäumen gesäumt, öffentlich zugänglich für alle. Drum herum reihen sich die Geschäfte aneinander. Es gibt Cafés, Restaurants und ein Kino. Hier wird kein Center auf die grüne Wiese gepflanzt – das Bauland war zuvor Brachfläche –, sondern die grüne Wiese auf das Center: Das Dach ist begrünt und zum Teil begehbar. „Meydan" heißt das

Gruen's mall became a success, and his principle was copied in many places. Today one sometimes hears that America has more shopping centres than schools. And in Europe too the success of the mall was celebrated. Admittedly, most of Gruen's imitators had primarily business interests in view, rather than the urban planning impetus by which Gruen had been driven. And so, many shopping centres became what the Austrian architect had been trying to avoid – single-function centres, in which, apart from the shopping experience, at best a little gastronomy and entertainment was offered, but these had the one and only purpose of encouraging people to buy. These centres, which often unite several retail businesses under one roof, without great architectural aspirations, no longer have social and integrative functions – or if they do, then only as a welcome side effect. So what was left of Gruen's idea was often only what Rem Koolhaas was later to call 'junk space' – heartlessly pieced-together structures with artificial light, windowless buildings that inexorably burrow their way with their escalators into the depths of the earth. And shopping, according to Koolhaas, was 'the only form of public life that remains to us'.

But back to Istanbul – or, more precisely, to Ümraniye. The history of this district on the Asian side of the city is symptomatic of Istanbul's growth in the last century. Until 1950 Ümraniye was still a small village on the edge of the city, which people in Istanbul knew at best only because they had to pass through it on their way to the resort of Sile on the Black Sea. The development plan of 1980 made no great plans for Ümraniye; rather, the shores of the Sea of Marmara – from Kadıköy via Bostancı to Maltepe and Kartal – were to be developed. Ümraniye had no great attraction for the city planners, since it offered neither an unobstructed view of the sea nor closeness to the historic centre on the European side, and instead only inhospitable terrain on high land. But what they had not realized at the time was that Ümraniye lies precisely between the access roads leading to the two bridges across the Bosphorus – one was opened in 1973, the other in 1988 – and thus between the essential arteries of the city. This location eventually made the area attractive for factories, company headquarters, residential buildings and department stores. Today Bosch, Bayer and Siemens, for example, have their headquarters here. As many people live in Ümraniye as in Düsseldorf, and today the district is among the fastest-growing in Istanbul – and the problems which the frantic pace of expansion brings with it have already been named: here too there is no centre to the periphery, no social areas for the community.

The METRO Group Asset Management is now attempting a solution to this problem. And what they are planning here in the middle of Ümraniye, between a motorway junction and proliferating residential buildings, is reminiscent of the visions of Victor Gruen. A shopping centre is coming into existence here that is to be much more than a supplier to the surrounding apartment blocks. A square is planned here, a sort of tree-lined piazza with public access to all, with rows of shops around it, as well as cafés, restaurants and a cinema. This is not a centre to be built on a green field – the site was formerly waste land – but rather a green area will be part of the centre: its roof is planted with greenery and partly accessible. This unusual

ungewöhnliche Einkaufszentrum, was aus dem Türkischen übersetzt so viel heißt wie „Platz". „Meydan", so das große Vorhaben der Planer, soll das neue Zentrum des Stadtteils werden.

Wie immer, wenn künstlich etwas kreiert werden soll, das anderswo organisch gewachsen ist, sind Zweifel angebracht. „Urbane Situationen entziehen sich der bewussten Gestaltung und können nur entstehen in einer historischen Entwicklung, die von keinem steuernden Zentrum dominiert wird", findet etwa der Stadtplaner und Architekturkritiker Dieter Hoffmann-Axthelm, der ähnliche Versuche analysiert hat. In der inszenierten Stadt werde Urbanität lediglich simuliert, deshalb bleibe sie letztlich immer steril – „es wird Stadt zitiert, nicht geschaffen." Die aufwendigste Inszenierung erreiche nun mal nicht „die Überzeugungskraft eines noch so windigen wirklichen Stadtzentrums". Doch hat „Meydan" nicht vielleicht das Potenzial, Kritiker eines Besseren zu belehren? Wird hier doch die Teilhabe weder an die Kaufkraft noch an die Öffnungszeiten gebunden. Außerhalb der Ladenzeile herrschen auch nicht die üblichen Verbote und totale Kontrolle. Stattdessen dürfen sich die Nachbarn auf dem begrünten Dach des Gebäudes sogar zum Picknick treffen. Auf dem Platz in der Mitte können Hochzeitsgesellschaften feiern oder sich die Jungs aus der Nachbarschaft zum Basketball treffen. Dürfte hier Gesellschaft nicht tatsächlich gelebt werden – statt nur gespielt?

Dass künstliche Plätze funktionieren, haben Architekten auf der ganzen Welt immerhin schon bewiesen. Allen voran der vertieft angelegte Platz des Rockefeller Centers in New York von den Architekten Raymond Hood, Harvey Wiley Corbett und Wallace K. Harrison. Der Platz ist ein Muss für jeden New York-Reisenden, ist das symbolische Herz der Metropole. Hier finden Konzerte statt, im Winter kann man Schlittschuh laufen. Kaum ein Tag vergeht, an dem den Passanten des Rockefeller Centers nicht etwas Besonderes geboten wird. An einem warmen Sommernachmittag gleiche der Platz „dem Treiben an Deck eines Schiffes – voller Leben, Sonne und Ferienstimmung", schrieb etwa der Sozialkritiker Frederick Lewis Allen einst in *Harper's*.

Was macht einen gelungenen Platz aus? Wenn man die Erkenntnisse der Experten studiert, dürfte das Erfolgsrezept in einer gesunden Mischung liegen, einer harmonischen Balance. So sieht etwa Adolfo Nodal im Abwechslungsreichtum eine zentrale Bedingung dafür, dass ein Platz ein lebhaftes Publikum anzieht. Nach Ansicht des New Yorker Designers und Architekten Emilio Ambasz sollte der Platz ein Gefühl der Zusammengehörigkeit erzeugen, gleichzeitig aber auch ein gewisses Maß an Abgeschlossenheit vermitteln. Und der Landschaftsplaner Lawrence Halprin findet, dass städtische Plätze sowohl aufregende Unterhaltung als auch Ruhe bieten sollten, beides jedoch räumlich voneinander getrennt.

Wird das Vorhaben in Ümraniye diesen Ansprüchen gerecht? Wie funktioniert der Platz als Handelsimmobilie? Schließlich geht es bei allen städteplanerischen Visionen natürlich auch um das Geschäft. Und wie wird die Nachbarschaft das Angebot aufnehmen? Ein halbes Jahr vor Eröffnung von „Meydan" gibt sich Prof. Michael Cesarz, Geschäftsführer der Immobiliengesellschaft METRO Group Asset Management, gespannt und neugierig: „Wir wollen es wagen, Seh- und Einkaufsgewohnheiten zu brechen, um Maßstäblichkeit in den Handel zurück zu bringen." Ob und wie sich das Konzept realisieren lässt, wie erst der Plan Gestalt annahm und dann der Platz sowie seine Gebäude, soll dieser Band dokumentieren.

"shopping square" is called "Meydan", a Turkish word meaning approximately a square or open space. Meydan, according to the planners' grand project, is to be the new centre of the district.

As always happens when something is to be artificially created that has elsewhere grown organically, doubts have been expressed. "Urban situations resist conscious design and can only come into existence in a historic development which is not dominated by any guiding centre," is the view for example of the urban planner and architectural critic Dieter Hoffmann-Axthelm, who has analysed similar attempts. In an artificial city, the argument runs, urban life is only simulated, and therefore ultimately always remains sterile – "a city is being quoted, not created." Even the most costly staging simply would not attain "the persuasive power of a real city centre, however unimaginative." But does Meydan not perhaps have the potential to teach its critics otherwise? Participation here, after all, is tied neither to purchasing power nor to opening times. Outside the line of shops there are not even the usual prohibitions and surveillance. Instead, neighbours can even meet for a picnic on the green roof of the building, the central square can be used for wedding parties, and there too the boys of the neighbourhood can play basketball. Surely a local community can really be experienced here, and not just simulated?

In any case, architects all over the world have already proved that artificial squares can work, in particular the sunken square of the Rockefeller Center in New York by the architects Raymond Hood, Harvey Wiley Corbett and Wallace K. Harrison. The square is a must for all travellers to New York; it is the symbolic heart of the Metropolis. Here concerts are held, and in winter one can go ice-skating. Hardly a day goes by on which something special is not offered to passers-by in the Rockefeller Center. On a warm summer afternoon the square is like "the deck of a ship – full of life, sunshine and holiday atmosphere", as the social critic Frederick Lewis Allen once wrote in *Harper's*.

What makes a successful square? When one studies the findings of the experts, the recipe for success should lie in a healthy mixture, a harmonious balance. Adolfo Nodal, for example, sees rich variety as a central condition for attracting a lively public to a square. In the view of the New York designer and architect Emilio Ambasz the square should create a sense of togetherness, but at the same time convey a certain measure of seclusion. Lawrence Halprin considers that urban squares should offer both exciting entertainment and restfulness, but the two should be spatially separated from each other.

Will the Ümraniye project fulfil these ambitions? How will the square function as a business property? And how will the neighbourhood receive the offer? Half a year before the opening of Meydan, Prof. Michael Cesarz, the managing director of the property company METRO Group Asset Management, appears excited and curious: "We dare to change habits of perception and of shopping, to bring back proportionateness into retail." Whether and how the concept is realized, how first the plan, and then the square and its buildings, first took shape, will be documented by this publication.

Von oben betrachtet erinnert der Große Basar in Istanbul an einen Karton mit Christbaumschmuck: Als hätte man 25 Kugeln ordentlich im Karree einsortiert – jeweils fünf in insgesamt drei Reihen. Nur fehlt der Glanz, stumpf ist die Oberfläche der steinernen Kuppeln. Funkeln und Glitzern gibt es dafür unter dem Dach reichlich. Von den hochkarätigen Auslagen der Juweliere und den schimmernden Stoffen der Tuchhändler geht es aus. Und von den glatten Marmorböden, die das einfallende Sonnenlicht sanft reflektieren. Selbst der Tee, den die Jungen hier auf silbernen Tabletts eilig durch das Gassenlabyrinth tragen, leuchtet bernsteingolden aus polierten Gläsern. Kein Wunder, dass flanierende Touristen hier zuweilen ein Leuchten in den Augen haben, das Kinder beim Anblick eines glitzernden Weihnachtsbaums bekommen – und in Erwartung großartiger Gaben.

Täglich kommen rund 150 000 Besucher zum Kapalı Çarşı, einem der größten überdachten Basare der Welt. Für rund 4 000 Geschäfte ist hier Platz. Doch nicht genug: In dem umgebenden Geflecht kleiner Gassen reiht sich ein Geschäft an das nächste. Wie eine Stadt in der Stadt liegt der Basar in Sultanahmet, dem historischen Zentrum Istanbuls. Hier – auf dem Hügel zwischen Goldenem Horn und Marmarameer – bauten die Griechen einst ihre Akropolis und später dann die berühmte Hagia Sophia. Als die Osmanen im 15. Jahrhundert die Stadt einnahmen, wurde die Kirche zur Moschee: Vier Minarette stellte man ihr an die Seiten. Gleich dahinter, da, wo die alte Akropolis stand, ließ der Sultan seinen Palast bauen. Und fast zeitgleich wie der Topkapı Sarayı, südlich in Laufweite davon, entstand auch der Basar.

Es war im Jahr 1461, acht Jahre nach seiner Eroberung der Stadt, als Sultan Mehmet I. den Bau eines Bedesten anordnete – eines bedeckten Basars nach dem Vorbild der großen Handelshallen in Edirne und Bursa. Samt und Seide, Gold und Gewürze sollten nicht mehr wie bisher auf offener Straße feilgeboten werden. Schließlich war Konstantinopel nun Hauptstadt des mächtigen Osmanischen Reiches. Da konnte man nicht länger Handel treiben, als wäre man in der Provinz. Der Basar, den der Sultan bauen ließ, war 1 300 Quadratmeter groß und hatte 15 große, acht kleine Kuppeln. Etwas später wurde er durch einen zweiten Bedesten ergänzt, den Sandal-Bedesten, der heute der Stadt gehört und für seine regelmäßigen Teppichversteigerungen berühmt ist. Um die beiden Markthallen herum entwickelten sich rund 60 Ladenstraßen mit knapp 30 Karawansereien, in denen die Händler ihre Lasttiere anbanden und eine Unterkunft für die Nacht fanden.

Bis ins 19. Jahrhundert war der Basar das wirtschaftliche Herz Istanbuls, überlebte Feuersbrünste und Erdbeben; unermüdlich wurden seine Mauern wieder hochgezogen. Erst mit dem Fin de Siècle verlor der Basar an Bedeutung: als die Händler übersiedelten auf das andere Ufer des Goldenen Horns, nach Eminönü und Beyoğlu, in die Nähe von neu eröffneten Banken. Heute ist es vor allem das Goldgeschäft, das die Händler wieder so unermüdlich in den Kapalı Çarşı zieht wie das einzigartige Flair die Touristen: 100 Tonnen dieses Edelmetalls gehen hier jährlich über den Ladentisch. Mehr als die Hälfte der Ladenbesitzer im Basar lebt direkt oder indirekt vom Gold.

VOM GROSSEN BASAR ZUM SHOPPING SQUARE
FROM THE GRAND BAZAAR TO THE SHOPPING SQUARE

Seen from above, the Grand Bazaar in Istanbul looks like a box of Christmas tree decorations: as though twenty-five balls had been placed in orderly fashion in a square formation – five to each of three rows. Only the shine is missing: the outer surface of the stone domes is dull. But under its roof, there is sparkle and glitter in abundance. It comes from the high-carat displays of the jewellers and the shimmering fabrics of the cloth merchants. And from the smooth marble floors, which gently reflect the sunlight that enters from above. Even the tea carried on silver trays by the boys who hurry through the labyrinth of alley-ways shines with an amber glow from polished glasses. No wonder that strolling tourists here have a gleam in their eyes, like that of children at the sight of a glittering Christmas tree – and in expectation of magnificent gifts.

Daily about 150,000 visitors come to the Kapalı Çarşı, one of the largest roofed bazaars in the world, with space for about four thousand businesses. But if that were not enough, in the surrounding network of little alleys more shops are lined up one next to the other. Like a city within the city, the bazaar lies in Sultanahmet, the historic centre of Istanbul. Here – on the hill between the Golden Horn and the Sea of Marmara – the Greeks once built their acropolis, and later the famous Hagia Sophia. When the Ottomans took over the city in the fifteenth century, the church became a mosque, with four minarets placed at its sides. Just behind it, where the old acropolis stood, the Sultan had his palace built. And at almost exactly the same time as the Topkapı Sarayı, to the south within walking distance of it, the bazaar too was created.

It was in 1461, eight years after his conquest of the city, that Sultan Mehmet II ordered the building of a bedesten – a covered bazaar on the model of the great trading halls of Edirne and Bursa. Velvet and silk, gold and spices were not to be offered for sale, as before, on the open street. After all, Constantinople was now the capital city of the mighty Ottoman empire. One could no longer buy and sell as though one were in the provinces. The bazaar that the Sultan had built was 1300 square metres in area and had fifteen large and eight small domes. Somewhat later it was supplemented by a second bedesten, the Sandal Bedesten, which today belongs to the city and is famous for its regular carpet auctions. Around the two market halls there developed about sixty shopping streets with some thirty-odd caravanserais, where the merchants tied up their pack-animals and found accommodation for the night.

Up to the nineteenth century the bazaar was the industrial heart of Istanbul, surviving fires and earthquakes, its walls tirelessly rebuilt. Only at the turn of the century did the bazaar lose in importance: when the dealers moved to the other shore of the Golden Horn, to Eminönü and Beyoğlu, near the newly opened banks. Today it is above all the trade in gold that draws the dealers back again so tirelessly to the Kapalı Çarşı, as well as the unique instinct of the tourists: one hundred tonnes of the precious metal annually cross the shop counters. More than half of the bazaar's shopkeepers live directly or indirectly from the sale of gold.

Auch wenn es in erster Linie um den Tausch von Ware gegen Geld geht: Der Basar ist mehr als ein Handelsplatz. Hier findet soziales Leben statt, wird nicht nur gefeilscht, sondern auch geplaudert, gegessen und gebetet, hier vergnügt man sich unter verzierten Kuppeln – und erledigt sogar noch so manche Besorgung. Heute gibt es auf dem Basar neben Cafés, Restaurants und Teeküchen auch eine Polizeistation, eine Post, Ärzte. Und in den Wechselstuben tauschten jahrelang nicht nur die Touristen ihr Urlaubsgeld, sondern – in Zeiten starker Inflation – auch die Einheimischen ihr Gehalt in harte Währung.

Wenn man so will, ist der Große Basar in Istanbul der Urtyp eines Shoppingcenters. Geschäfte und Gastronomie, Plätze zum Verweilen und die eine oder andere Institution der Infrastruktur – alles findet sich vom Wetter geschützt unter einem Dach. Und in der Tat ist der Basar durch seine strenge Trennung von Wohnen und Wirtschaften eine kulturelle Leistung der islamischen Welt. Indes: Das Prinzip Shoppingcenter, wie man es heute kennt, musste erst über den Umweg Amerika nach Istanbul kommen.

Der Ministerpräsident Turgut Özal soll die Idee von einer Texas-Reise mitgebracht haben. Angetan von der Houston Galleria mit ihrem spektakulären Atrium und einer Schlittschuhbahn neben allerlei Geschäften und Restaurants, veranlasste er nach seiner Rückkehr den Bau eines ebensolchen Konsum- und Entertainment-Tempels in Istanbul. Stolz eröffnete er im Jahr 1987 die Galeria Ataköy in der Nähe des Flughafens Atatürk, in der man ganz nach dem amerikanischen Muster so gut einkaufen wie eislaufen konnte – und die wiederum bald Vorbild sein sollte für eine Reihe weiterer Malls in Istanbul.

Die Galeria Ataköy ist ein Shoppingcenter der so genannten „ersten Generation". Ein großer, schachtelartiger Baukörper wird in den städtischen Raum gestellt – und die unmittelbare Umgebung weitestgehend ignoriert. Lediglich die Verkehrsnetze und Wegebeziehungen der Stadt, quasi die lebensnotwendigen Arterien der Mall, spielen bei Planung und Entwurf eine Rolle. Die äußere Erscheinung ist wenig bemerkenswert, innere Werte zählen mehr: Glatte Böden und Spiegel, glitzernde Wasserfontänen und verheißungsvolle Schaufensterauslagen schaffen im Inneren des Gebäudes eine freundliche, saubere und sichere Konsumwelt, die sich selbst genügt und von ihrem Umfeld stark abgrenzt.

Highlight des Gebäudes ist das obligatorische Glasdach. Der Blick auf den Himmel darf in keinem Shoppingcenter fehlen, ist es doch nach Victor Gruens Ansatz das Anliegen der Mall, ein Stadtzentrum zu imitieren, und dieses liegt, nach mitteleuropäischem Vorbild, unter freiem Himmel. Das Licht fällt aber nicht einfach so in den Raum, es wird – mittels Spiegel- und Wasseroberflächen, Schaufenstern und blank polierter Böden – gebrochen, vervielfacht, umgelenkt und obendrein durch gezielt eingesetztes künstliches Licht ergänzt. Dadurch ist immer so viel Helligkeit vorhanden, dass auch mal ein trübes Wetter nicht auf die Stimmung der Kunden schlägt.

Doch nicht nur Wind und Regen kann man in der blitzblanken Konsumoase ausblenden: Nichts erinnert an die sozialen Schieflagen und Probleme der Stadt, an Arbeitslosigkeit, Armut und Kriminalität. Die Security-Maßnahmen an den Eingängen, eine Antwort auf die verheerenden Terroranschläge der PKK-Anhänger auf Gebäude und Plätze in Istanbul, verstärken noch das Gefühl der Sicherheit und Abschottung. Wie an einem Flughafen fühlt sich der Kunde, dessen Körper in der Lichtschranke durchleuchtet wird wie seine Taschen auf dem Gepäckband. Start frei also für einen Freiflug in eine bessere Welt – ohne schlechtes Wetter und ohne Sorgen, wo die Menschen freundlich sind und das Vergnügen wartet. Nur zu gern folgen die Istanbuler diesem unausgesprochenen Ausruf: Am Sonntag zieht es inzwischen mehr Familien in die Mall als ans Meer.

Even if it is primarily a matter of the exchanging of wares for money, the bazaar is more than a trading area. Here social life is conducted, here people come not only to haggle but also to chat, eat and pray, enjoy themselves under the ornate domes – and carry out all sorts of other errands. Today the bazaar also contains not only cafés, restaurants and tea shops, but also a police station, a post office, and doctors' surgeries. And in the bureaux de change, all year round, not only do the tourists change their holiday money, but – in times of severe inflation – the locals also convert their income into hard currency.

The Grand Bazaar in Istanbul is, if you like, the archetype of a shopping centre; shops and gastronomy, places to linger and one institution or other of the infrastructure all under one roof, protected from the weather. And in fact the bazaar, with its strict separation of dwelling from trading, is a cultural achievement of the Islamic world. However, the shopping centre principle, as we know it today, had to come to Istanbul only by way of America.

The prime minister, Turgut Özal, is said to have brought the idea back from a trip to Texas. Much taken by the Houston Galleria with its spectacular atrium and an ice rink as well as all sorts of shops and restaurants, on his return he organized the building of a similar temple of consumer goods and entertainment. In 1987 he proudly opened the Galeria Ataköy near the Atatürk airport, where, just as in the American model, one could go shopping or ice-skating – and which was in its turn to be the model for a series of further malls in Istanbul.

Galeria Ataköy is a shopping centre of the so-called 'first generation': a large, box-like structure placed in the urban space, largely ignoring the immediate surroundings. Only the traffic networks and street connections of the city, as it were, the essential arteries of the mall, played a part in its planning and design. Its outward appearance is unremarkable, inner values counting for more: smooth floors and mirrors, glittering fountains and tempting window displays in the interior of the building create a friendly, clean and safe consumer world, which is sufficient to itself and strictly demarcated from its surroundings.

The highlight of the building is the requisite glass roof. A view of the sky is indispensable in any shopping centre; after all, according to Victor Gruen's principles, the mall's business is to imitate a city centre, and this one, following the central European model, lies in the open air. But light does not fall at random into the space; by means of mirror and water surfaces, display windows and floors polished to a high sheen, it is broken up, multiplied, diverted and in addition supplemented by carefully directed artificial light. The result is so much brightness that even occasional dull weather cannot affect the mood of the customers.

But it is not only wind and rain that can be faded out in this sparklingly clean consumer oasis: there is nothing to remind one of the social imbalances and problems of the city, of unemployment, poverty and crime. The security measures at the entrances, a response to the devastating terrorist attacks of the PKK (Kurdish separatist) supporters on buildings and squares in Istanbul, only serve to strengthen the sense of safety and seclusion. The customer, when his body is X-rayed in the photoelectric beam, feels as though at an airport, when his luggage is put on the carousel. All clear then for a free flight into a better world – one without bad weather or worries, where people are friendly and pleasure awaits. Only too eagerly do the people of Istanbul follow this unspoken call: On Sundays, more families are drawn to the mall than to the beach.

Die Anordnung der Geschäfte in der Galeria erfolgte nach dem Dumbbell-Prinzip. Das heißt so, weil der ursprüngliche Grundriss von oben betrachtet einem Knochen (englisch: dumbbell) ähnelt: mit den beiden „Ankern" – großflächige Geschäfte, die wegen ihrer Marktposition oder Attraktivität die Grundfrequenz im Shoppingcenter steigern – als Schwerpunkte an den Enden einer linearen Shopzeile. Das Prinzip ist so alt wie die Malls Amerikas: Victor Gruen hatte es in seinem 1956 entworfenen Southdale Center eingeführt. Nur sind es in der Galeria nicht mehr nur zwei, sondern drei Anker; die Houston Galleria in Texas hat sogar insgesamt fünf.

Der Shop-Mix lässt kaum Wünsche offen. Nahezu alles, wonach der Verbraucher begehren kann, ist unter einem Dach und in wenigen Schritten zu erreichen. Für Istanbul alles andere als gewöhnlich: Stehen Waren unterschiedlicher Produktgattungen auf dem Einkaufszettel, muss man hier nämlich oft große Distanzen überwinden. Weite Teile der Stadt, und beispielsweise auch der Basar, sind noch nach dem Zunftwesen sortiert. Ähnlich wie einst in Mitteleuropa, wo jahrhundertelang die Berufsgruppen in einer bestimmten Straße – der Handwerkergasse, der Gerbergasse etc. – zu finden waren, nur dass es sich in Istanbul nicht um kleine Gassen handelt, die unmittelbar aneinanderstoßen, sondern um gewaltige Areale, jeweils mitunter so groß wie das Zentrum einer deutschen Kleinstadt. Man muss nur einmal im Istanbuler Viertel Beyoğlu vor dem Galataturm nach rechts laufen und schon reiht sich bald ein Elektrikerladen an den nächsten, etwas weiter ist die Auswahl an Lampen und Lüstern überwältigend und am Fuße des Hügels, nahe dem Goldenen Horn, gibt es so viel Klempner- und Sanitärbedarf auf einmal zu sehen wie in keinem noch so großen Baumarkt der Welt. Fazit: Wer hier nur drei Produkte aus verschiedenen Bereichen kaufen möchte, ist schon mal einen ganzen Tag unterwegs.

Auch der Einkauf von Bekleidung kann zum langen Fußmarsch werden: Ganze zwei Kilometer lang ist die Istiklal Caddesi, die Haupteinkaufsstraße in Taksim. Für fußmüde Passanten wurde schon Anfang des letzten Jahrhunderts eine Straßenbahnlinie mitten auf den Boulevard gesetzt – doch so oft kann die kleine historische Bahn kaum fahren, dass ihr einziger Wagen alle mitzunehmen vermag, die nicht mehr laufen möchten. Das Shoppingcenter als ein Gebäude, in dem nahezu sämtliche Gebrauchs- und Konsumwaren in verschiedenen Preisklassen fußläufig erreichbar sind und Rolltreppen den Kunden einen Teil des Weges abnehmen, musste demnach unweigerlich zum Erfolg führen. Und noch etwas spricht für die Mall in der Metropole: Seitdem immer mehr türkische Frauen arbeiten und sich vom traditionellen islamischen Frauenbild lösen, steigt auch der Bedarf an sicheren und vielfältigen Einkaufsmöglichkeiten nach Feierabend.

Nicht lange, und die Galeria bekam Konkurrenz. Heute ist die Stadt für ihre Malls fast so berühmt wie für ihre Moscheen. Sogar das größte Shoppingcenter Europas findet man in Istanbul: das Cevahir Shopping Center in Şişli entworfen von Minoru Yamasaki & Associates, dem Büro des Architekten des World Trade Centers in New York. Auf einem alten Busdepot sollte ein ähnlicher Gebäudekomplex entstehen wie der in New York – jedoch mit drei Wolkenkratzern, 40 und 48 Stockwerke hoch, und einem Shoppingcenter in den unteren sechs Stockwerken. Doch dann dauerte es allein acht Jahre, um die Mall zu beenden, sodass man es schließlich dabei beließ. 620 000 Quadratmeter ist die Megamall groß und damit so weitläufig,

The arrangement of the shops in the Galeria follows the dumb-bell principle because the original ground plan, seen from above, resembles a dumb-bell, with its two 'anchors' – extensive shops that because of their market position or attractiveness increase the fundamental frequency in the shopping centre – as main focus points at the ends of a linear row of shops. The principle is as old as America's malls; Victor Gruen introduced it in his Southdale Center in 1956. But in the Galeria there are no longer only two but three anchors; the Houston Galleria in Texas has as many as five in all.

The mix of shops leaves hardly anything to be desired. Just about anything the consumer might wish is to be found under one roof and within a few steps. Istanbul is anything but ordinary: If your shopping list includes products of different types, you can here expect to have to cover great distances. Large areas of the city, and of the bazaar too, are still organized on the guild principle, just as formerly in central Europe, where for centuries the professional groups were each to be found in a certain street – the craftsmen's street, the tanners' street, and so on – except that in Istanbul it is not a case of small alleys, but of huge areas, each sometimes as large as the centre of a small town in northern Europe. You only have to turn right once in the Beyoğlu district of Istanbul, at the Galata tower, and already one electrical shop follows another, further on the choice of lamps and chandeliers is overwhelming, and at the foot of the hill, near the Golden Horn, there are suddenly more plumbers' and sanitary appliance shops to be seen at once than in any of the world's builders' markets. As a result, if you want to buy just three products of different genres, it can easily take you a whole day.

Buying clothes, too, can turn into a long foot-slog. The Istiklal Caddesi, the main shopping street in Taksim, is a whole two kilometres long. As early as the beginning of the last century, a tramline was placed in the middle of the boulevard for foot-weary shoppers – but this historic little line can hardly make as many journeys as would be needed for its single carriage to accommodate everyone who is tired of walking. The shopping centre, as a building in which nearly all consumer goods in various price ranges are accessible on foot and escalators take away the burden of part of the journey, could as a result only be an inevitable success. And one more factor speaks in favour of the mall in the metropolis: since more and more Turkish women go out to work and are freeing themselves from the traditional Islamic image of women, the demand has risen for shopping opportunities in an atmosphere of security and variety after finishing work.

Soon the Galeria encountered competition. Today the city is almost as well known for its malls as its mosques. Even the largest shopping centre in Europe is to be found in Istanbul: the Cevahir Shopping Center in the Şişli district designed by Minoru Yamasaki & Associates, the architectural firm that created the World Trade Center in New York. On the site of an old bus garage, a complex of buildings was to be created similar to the one in New York – but with three skyscrapers, 40 and 48 storeys high, and a shopping centre on the lower six storeys. But then it took eight years just to complete the mall, so that in the end it was left at that. This mega-mall is 620,000 square metres in area, and so extensive that the advantage of short

dass der oben genannte Vorteil der kurzen Wege hier kaum noch zutrifft. Doch die rund 50 000 Besucher, die täglich herkommen, arrangieren sich damit, schätzen die große Auswahl aus 280 Geschäften – genau doppelt so viele, wie die Galeria hat – ebenso wie aus dem umfangreichen Programm der 13 Kinos. In dem Atrium des Gebäudes finden oft auch Konzerte statt: Dann verwandelt sich der Springbrunnen in eine Hebebühne, sodass die Stars und Sternchen auch zu denen kommen, die in den oberen Stockwerken auf der Balustrade jubeln.

Wenige Metrostationen weiter und man ist in einer Shopping Mall, die weniger durch ihre Größe, vielmehr durch ihr Design für Aufsehen sorgt. An die Architektur von Frank Lloyd Wright wird unweigerlich erinnert, wer den Eingang von Kanyon Istanbul passiert. Zwar schieben sich hier keine Rampen spiralförmig in die Höhe, vielmehr verlaufen die Balustraden horizontal über vier Stockwerke an den Geschäften entlang. Auch bewegt sich der Besucher nicht in einem geschlossenen, sondern in einem offenen Raum. Er flaniert in den einzelnen Stockwerken in einem Arkadengang vor Regen geschützt, ist aber dennoch an der frischen Luft. Das Shopping-Gefühl von Nişantaşı, dem feinen Einkaufsviertel Istanbuls, wo sich eine schicke Boutique an die andere reiht, soll hier imitiert werden.

Damit weder Hitze noch Kälte den Bummel beeinträchtigen, wurde eine weltweit einzigartige Klimaanlage installiert: Die offenen Räume werden mit Luft ventiliert, dadurch entsteht eine unsichtbare „thermostatische Schutzwand". Vor den Winden, die durch das Ensemble – das aufgrund seiner steilen Bauweise Kanyon genannt wird – besonders stark wehen, dürfte diese jedoch kaum schützen. Im besten Fall wirkt es umsatzfördernd, wenn sich die Menschen vor dem Wind in die Geschäfte flüchten. Im schlimmsten Fall bleiben sie bei bestimmten Wetterlagen einfach weg.

Die bewusste Abwendung vom geschlossenen, wetterunabhängigen Shoppingcenter, die das Büro von Jon Jerde, dem weltweit erfolgreichsten Architekt für Einkaufs- und Erlebniszentren – The Jerde Partnership of Los Angeles –, in Kooperation mit dem türkischen Architekturbüro Tabanlıoğlu mit Kanyon verfolgt hat, muss als mutig bezeichnet werden. Mit einem Shoppingcenter der ersten Generation wie das Galeria und die meisten anderen Center in Istanbul hat das im Mai 2006 eröffnete Kanyon nicht viel zu tun. Mit der 37 500 Quadratmeter großen Mall und dem dazugehörenden Büroturm über 30 Stockwerke, dem Hochhaus mit Wohnungen auf 22 Etagen und dem imposanten Kinokomplex mit neun Sälen haben Jerde und Tabanlıoğlu einen Generationenwechsel eingeläutet.

Und die Entwicklung geht weiter. 34 Shoppingcenter gibt es in Istanbul derzeit, rund 20 sind im Bau, weitere 20 in Planung. Die Konkurrenz unter den Centern ist groß, jedes versucht auf seine Art, einzigartig zu sein. Das Capitol zum Beispiel lockt mit einem besonders großen Kinokomplex; das Tepe Carrefour wiederum hat sich ganz der Nautik verschrieben: Kleine Haie schwimmen in großen Becken zwischen den Shops. Und nun möchte die METRO Group Asset Management eine weitere Mall bauen – ähnlich wie Kanyon ebenfalls ein offenes Center: mit den genannten Risiken und mit rund 70 000 Quadratmetern Fläche ebenfalls nicht eines der größten. Da bedarf es – neben eines besonderen Konzepts bezüglich Zielgruppe und Mietermix – vor allem eines außergewöhnlichen Entwurfs, um neben der Konkurrenz bestehen zu können. Und dieser musste erst gefunden werden.

journeys mentioned above hardly applies here any more. But the visitors, around 50,000 in number, who come here daily put up with this, appreciate the great choice of 280 shops – exactly twice as many as in the Galeria – as much as the comprehensive range of films offered by the thirteen cinemas. In the atrium of the building, concerts are often performed too, when the fountain is transformed into a hydraulic ramp, so that the stars and starlets also come to those applauding from the upper storeys on the balustrade.

A few Metro stations further on, and we are in a shopping mall which impresses less by its size than by its design. Anyone passing the entrance to Kanyon Istanbul is inevitably reminded of the architecture of Frank Lloyd Wright. Admittedly, here there are no ramps rising in spirals, rather the balustrades run horizontally across four storeys along the shops. Moreover, the visitor does not move in a closed but in an open space. He strolls through the individual storeys, protected from rain by an arcade, but is still in the fresh air. The intention here is to recreate the shopping atmosphere of Nişantaşı, the up-market shopping district of Istanbul, where one chic boutique follows another.

So that neither heat nor cold adversely affects the stroll, an air-conditioning system unique throughout the world was installed. The open spaces are ventilated with fresh air, producing an invisible 'thermostatic protective wall'. But these can hardly protect against the winds that blow with particular strength through the complex, which is known as the Kanyon on account of its steep building structure. At best it makes for a high sales turnover when people flee from the wind into the shops, where they buy things they had not actually been looking for. But in the worst case, under certain weather conditions they simply stay away.

The conscious move away from the closed shopping centre, independent of the weather, that has been pursued with the Kanyon by the office of Jon Jerde, the most successful architect in the world in the area of shopping and experience centres – The Jerde Partnership of Los Angeles – in cooperation with the Turkish architectural firm of Tabanlioğlu, must be considered as a brave move. Opened in May 2006, the Kanyon does not have much in common with a shopping centre of the first generation like the Galeria and most of the other centres in Istanbul. With this mall, 37,500 square metres in area, and the office tower attached to it of over 30 storeys, the high-rise apartment building on 22 floors and the impressive cinema complex with nine screens, Jerde and Tabanlioğlu have inaugurated a generational change.

And the development goes on. At present there are 34 shopping centres in Istanbul, about 20 under construction, and a further 20 at the planning stage. Competition is lively among the centres, each trying to be unique in its own way. The Capitol, for example, offers the temptation of a particularly large cinema complex, while the Tepe Carrefour on the other hand has dedicated itself entirely to the nautical theme: Small sharks swim in the large pool between the shops. And now the METRO Group Asset Management is planning a shopping square – like the Kanyon, an open centre; with the risks mentioned above, and with an area of about 70,000 square metres, also not one of the largest. To be able to assert itself against the competition, it therefore needed – apart from a special concept in terms of target group and mix of tenants – above all an exceptional design And this had still to be found.

Wer ein Gebäude plant, schreibt für gewöhnlich einen Architektenwettbewerb aus und sucht aus den eingereichten Entwürfen den besten aus, um ihn zu realisieren. Das Verfahren garantiert dem Bauherrn eine vergleichsweise große Auswahl bei überschaubarem Aufwand. Der Nachteil jedoch: Er hat weder Einblick in die Entwicklung des Entwurfs noch Einfluss darauf. Nachbesserungen am Siegerentwurf gehören somit zum Geschäft und sind für Architekten wie Bauherrn oft so unerfreulich wie aufwendig. Auf der Suche nach dem optimalen Entwurf für ihr Grundstück in Ümraniye beschritt die METRO Group Asset Management daher einen anderen, etwas ungewöhnlichen Weg.

Es war im März 2005, als im Hotel Conrad im Istanbuler Stadtteil Beşiktaş – der für den gleichnamigen Fußballclub ebenso bekannt ist wie für den pompösen Sultanspalast Dolmabahçe – ein halbes Dutzend namhafter, international tätiger Architekten eincheckten. Aus Hamburg zum Beispiel war Hadi Teherani von Bothe Richter Teherani (BRT Architekten) angereist. Das Büro hatte unter anderem den Fernbahnhof Frankfurt-Flughafen entworfen und die Twin Towers in Dubai. Für die Europa-Passage in Hamburg gab es im Jahr 2007 auf der Internationalen Immobilienmesse Mipim in Cannes den begehrten Mipim Award. Das Team um Teherani gilt als Experte auf dem Gebiet, den öffentlichen Raum in der Fläche neu zu entwickeln. Mit ihren Werken schaffen sie Identitätspunkte im urbanen Raum. „Wie Choreografen geht es ihnen um die menschlichen Bewegungen in der Stadt", schrieb der Architekturkritiker Klaus-Dieter Weiss einmal.

Aus Frankfurt kamen Mitarbeiter von J.S.K. Architekten. Das Büro wurde 1961 von Helmut W. Joos gegründet und machte mit repräsentativen Großprojekten wie dem Flughafen Frankfurt/Main oder Düsseldorf Airport 2000 auf sich aufmerksam. Im Team in Istanbul dabei waren Jurek M. Slapa und Wolfgang Marcour, die unter anderem den Neubau für das Stilwerk Düsseldorf entwarfen. Das Gebäude, welches vom Bund Deutscher Architekten Düsseldorf ausgezeichnet wurde, erhebt sich in fünf Etagen über einem elliptischen Grundriss und endet in 32 Meter Höhe in einem Glasdach, welches geöffnet werden kann – „Haus mit Himmel" wird das Gebäude auch genannt.

Aus London reisten Chris Lanksbury und John Evans von Chapman Taylor an. Das 1959 gegründete Büro hat – neben verschiedenen Büro-, Verwaltungs- oder Flughafenbauten wie etwa den Terminal Süd von Gatwick – zahlreiche Einkaufscenter entworfen, welche bei den Preisverleihungen des International Council of Shopping Centers (ICSC) nahezu ständig unter den ersten Plätzen zu finden sind. Whitefriars in Canterbury zum Beispiel: Hier wurde aus einem ehemaligen Klosterareal ein neuer Stadtteil mit vielen Geschäften und neuen Plätzen – Einkaufsvergnügen unter freiem Himmel und in historischer Kulisse. Für Düsseldorf entwarfen Chapman Taylor die Schadow Arkaden und die Kö-Galerie.

DER ARCHITEKTURWETTBEWERB
THE ARCHITECTURAL COMPETITION

Someone who is planning a building usually sets up an architectural competition and chooses the best among the designs submitted in order to realize it. This procedure guarantees the client a comparatively wide choice at reasonable expense. The disadvantage, however, is that he has neither any insight into the development of the design, nor influence upon it. Improvements to the winning design are thus part of the deal and are for both architects and client often as unpleasant as they are costly. In the search for the best design for their site in Ümraniye, therefore, METRO Group Asset Management struck out a different, somewhat unusual path.

It was in March 2005 that half a dozen notable internationally active architects checked into the Hotel Conrad in the Beşiktaş district of Istanbul, known as much for the football club of the same name as for its grandiose sultan's palace of Dolmabahçe. Hadi Teherani, for example, had arrived from Hamburg, representing Bothe Richter Teherani (BRT Architekten). This firm had designed among other buildings the main-line railway station Frankfurt-Flughafen and the Twin Towers in Dubai. For the Europa Passage in Hamburg in 2007 it had won the coveted Mipim Award at Mipim, the World's Property Market, in Cannes. Teherani's team are considered experts in the field of new developments for public spaces. With their works they create identity points in the urban space. "Like choreographers, they are concerned with human movement in the city," the architectural critic Klaus-Dieter Weiss once wrote.

From Frankfurt came representatives from JSK Architekten, a firm founded in 1961 by Helmut W. Joos which has drawn attention to itself with impressive major projects such as the Frankfurt/Main airport and 'Düsseldorf Airport 2000'. The team sent to Istanbul included Jurek M. Slapa and Wolfgang Marcour, who designed, for example, the new building for the Stilwerk complex in Düsseldorf. This building, which received an award from the Society of German Architects in Düsseldorf, rises to 32 metres in five storeys above an elliptical ground plan, ending in a glass roof, which can be opened – the building has been called the 'House with a Heaven'.

From London, Chris Lanksbury and John Evans came from Chapman Taylor, a firm founded in 1959, which, apart from various office, administration and airport buildings such as the Gatwick South Terminal, has designed numerous shopping centres. These are almost continuously to be found taking first place at the award ceremonies of the International Council of Shopping Centers (ICSC) – for example Whitefriars in Canterbury, where a former monastery was transformed into a new city district with many shops and new squares – shopping enjoyment in the open air and in a historic setting. For Düsseldorf, Chapman Taylor designed the Schadow Arcades and the Kö-Galerie.

Charakteristisch für den Entwurf der METRO
Group Asset Management: Das Kino als
Landmark (Abbildung links und rechts oben)
und die Verzahnung des Gebäudekomplexes
mit dem urbanen Kontext (Abbildung rechts
unten)
Typical of METRO Group Asset Management
design: the cinema as a landmark (left and
above right) and the interweaving of the
building complex into the urban context
(below right)

cinema
real,-
IKEA
real,-

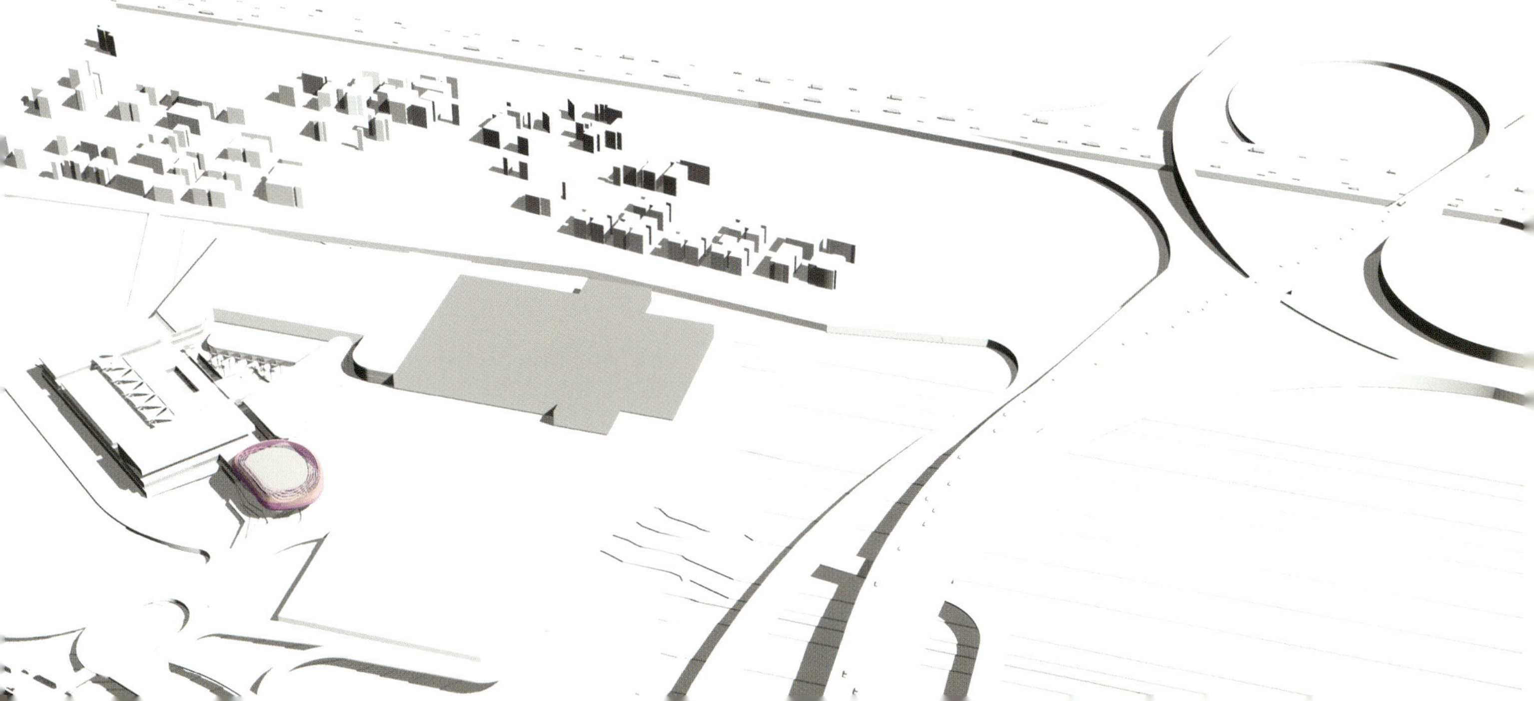

Ebenfalls aus London kamen die Architekten von Foreign Office Architects (FOA). Es sind seine außergewöhnlichen urbanen Landschaften, für die das junge Büro um die Gründer Alejandro Zaera Polo und Farshid
Moussavi – die nach Lehrjahren bei Rem Koolhaas als Lehrer an der Londoner Architectural Association
wirkten – bekannt ist. In der Architekturszene sorgten sie etwa mit ihrem „Blue Moon"-Gebäude in Groningen, dem Stadttheater in Torrevieja in Spanien und nicht zuletzt mit dem Yokohama International Ferry
Terminal südlich von Tokio für Aufsehen. Für die Olympischen Spiele in London 2012 gehören FOA zu dem
Team, das den Olympiapark im Herzen der Stadt entwirft. Inzwischen gelten FOA als Vertreter jener führenden Generation junger Architekten, die eine Neuorientierung in Theorie und Praxis bewirkt haben. Was das
Büro, in Istanbul vertreten durch Friedrich Ludewig, Kenichi Matsuzawa und Kitai Hikaru, außer ihrem un-
gewöhnlichen Ansatz und seiner jungen Geschichte von den anderen angereisten Architekten unterschied:
Ein Shoppingcenter hatte es bis dato noch nicht entworfen.
Keinen weiten Weg hatten immerhin die Architekten von Tabanlioğlu, dem führenden Architektenbüro
der Türkei mit Sitz in Istanbul. Sie standen schon dem amerikanischen Architekten John Simones von
Jerde Partnership International aus Los Angeles bei der Ausführung des Entwurfs für das spektakuläre Ein-
kaufscenter Kanyon im Stadtteil Levent zur Seite. In Istanbul wird bis 2009 der von Tabanlioğlu entworfene
Wolkenkratzer „Sapphire of Istanbul" gebaut, welcher neben Wohnungen und Büros auch eine 35 000
Quadratmeter große Mall beherbergt. Mit seinen 54 Stockwerken und einer Höhe von 261 Metern wird es
das zweithöchste Gebäude des Landes; das erste ökologische Hochhaus der Türkei ist es auch: mit einer
speziellen Klimaanlage und eigenen Gärten auf jedem dritten Stockwerk.
Die Aufgabe für die fünf eingeladenen Architektenteams: Innerhalb der nächsten drei Tage sollten sie jeweils einen Prototypen für eine Mall entwickeln, die auf dem Grundstück von METRO Group Asset Management neben dem bereits eröffneten Ikea-Möbelhaus gebaut wird. Die Wünsche des Bauherrn hatten
die Architekten schon im Gepäck. Ein urbanes Entertainment-Center für Ümraniye sollte das neue Gebäude werden – ein Ort, an dem sich die Menschen gern treffen und für eine Weile bleiben möchten. Die Architektur sollte außergewöhnlich sein und nichts zu tun haben mit der Kastenform der sogenannten ersten
Generation von Shoppingcentern. Oder kurz gesagt: Nichts Geringeres wünschten sich die Planer als die
Architektur für eine neue Art Mall in Istanbul.
Zu den einzelnen Vorgaben: Das neue Gebäude geht nur über zwei Stockwerke und ist insgesamt bis zu
12,5 Meter hoch, jedoch dürfe bei einigen Gebäudeteilen und wenn die Architektur es erfordert – wie etwa
beim Kinokomplex – diese Höhe überschritten werden. Mindestens 2500 Parkplätze müssen geschaffen
werden. Gewünscht wurde eine deutliche Abgrenzung zwischen den individuellen Gebäudeteilen: Das
Center sollte übersichtlich und leicht zugänglich sein. Die einzelnen Shops werden zu Themenbereichen
zusammengefasst und diese miteinander verbunden. Das Gebäude muss sich in den umliegenden Wohn-

Also from London came the architects from Foreign Office Architects (FOA). This young firm with its founders Alejandro Zaera Polo und Farshid Moussavi, who, after years of study with Rem Kohlhaas, were active as teachers at the London Architectural Association, is known for its exceptional urban landscapes. On the architectural scene they attracted attention with, for example, their 'Blue Moon' building in Groningen, the city theatre in Torrevieja in Spain, and not least the Yokohama International Ferry Terminal, south of Tokyo. For the 2012 Olympic Games in London, FOA are among the team designing the Olympic Park in the heart of the city. Meanwhile, FOA are part of that leading generation of young architects who have brought about a new orientation in theory and practice. What differentiated the firm, represented in Istanbul by Friedrich Ludewig, Kenichi Matsuzawa and Kitai Hikaru, apart from its unique approach and its brief history, from the other visiting architects, was that they had never before designed a shopping centre.

The architects from Tabanlioğlu, the leading architectural firm in Turkey, at least did not have far to come, as their office is in Istanbul. They had already worked alongside the American architect John Simones of Jerde Partnership International from Los Angeles in executing the design for the spectacular Canyon shopping centre in the Levent district of the city. In Istanbul, the 'Sapphire of Istanbul' skyscraper designed by Tabanlioğlu is to be built by 2009, including, as well as apartments and offices, a mall of 35,000 square metres in area. With its 54 storeys and height of 261 metres it will be the second tallest building in the country; it will also be Turkey's first ecological high-rise, with a special air-conditioning system and gardens on every third storey.

The task for each of the five invited architectural teams was to design within the next three days a prototype for a mall, which is to be built on the METRO Group Asset Management site next to the IKEA furniture store already opened there. The architects were already aware of their client's requirements and had brought them along. The new building was to be an urban entertainment centre for Ümraniye – a place where people would enjoy meeting and lingering for a while. The architecture should be unusual and have nothing in common with the box shapes of the so-called first generation of shopping centres. In short, the planners wanted nothing less than the architecture for a new kind of mall in Istanbul.

As far as detailed guidelines are concerned, the new building is to have only two storeys and reach a total height of up to 12.5 metres, but with some parts of the building, and if the architecture demands it – for example with the cinema complex – this height may be exceeded. At least 2,500 parking spaces must be created. A clear demarcation between the individual parts of the building is required: the centre must be clearly laid out and easily accessible. The individual shops will be grouped together in themed areas and these will be linked with each other. The building must be integrated in the surrounding residential area as well as the environs of IKEA, and directly accessible. As much daylight as possible should enter the building. The client also laid great value on a distinctive design for the façades.

bezirk integrieren sowie in das Umfeld von Ikea – und direkt zugänglich sein. Es sollte so viel Tageslicht wie möglich in den Komplex dringen. Großen Wert legten die Bauherren auch auf eine außergewöhnliche Gestaltung der Fassaden.

Vor allem eine Idee sollten die Architekten in ihre Überlegungen einbinden: Könnten die einzelnen Gebäudeteile nicht um einen zentralen Platz gruppiert werden – um eine Art Marktplatz als zentralen Punkt, als Verbindungselement mit Springbrunnen, Bäumen und Sträuchern? Ein öffentlicher Raum könnte hier entstehen, nutzbar für erholsame Kaffeepausen und Sport, für Märkte und Veranstaltungen. Von dem Platz aus, so gehen die Überlegungen weiter, könnte zum Beispiel auch der Zugang zu einem unterirdischen Parksystem erfolgen. Dass die gewünschten Kriterien durchaus zu realisieren sind, hatten die Architekten von METRO Group Asset Management bereits selbst bewiesen: Monate vor dem Workshop wurde von ihnen ein Entwurf erarbeitet. Das Kino als Landmark sowie die Position der einzelnen Retailwelten waren hier ebenso dargestellt wie die Verzahnung des Gebäudekomplexes mit der ihn umgebenden Stadt.

Was den angereisten Architekten neben diesem Modell bei ihrer Arbeit helfen sollte: eine Führung über drei ausgewählte Shoppingcenter Istanbuls – Metro City, Akmerkez und das in unmittelbarer Nachbarschaft gelegene Carrefour – sowie über das zu bebauende Gelände. Jedes Team bekam einen eigenen Salon im Business-Bereich des Hotels, alle notwendigen Materialien sowie die technischen Voraussetzungen für eine Standleitung zu den Kollegen in den Büros in London, Hamburg, Frankfurt und Istanbul.

Bereits am Abend des zweiten Tages wurden die Architekten gebeten, erste Ideen zu präsentieren. Das Team von BRT zum Beispiel zeigte, wie es zunächst die Überlegung des Bauherrn aufgriff und einen Platz in der Mitte vorsah, um den sich alle anderen Gebäudeteile anordneten. Die Architekten von JSK hingegen präferierten zunächst eine modulare Struktur: Statt eines oder mehrerer großer Gebäudeteile stellten sie sich viele kleine vor, die sich zum Teil zu größeren zusammenfügen. Mit dieser kleinteiligen Struktur wollten sie auf die fragmentarische Bebauung im nahen Umfeld des Geländes reagieren. Auch Chapman Taylor sowie Tabanlıoğlu skizzierten erste Überlegungen zur Gebäudestruktur. Nur FOA machten eine Ausnahme und überraschten damit, statt eines Gebäudes lediglich sämtliche analysierten Wegebeziehungen aufzuzeichnen. Von einem Shoppingcenter war nichts zu sehen. Auch bei der zweiten Präsentation am nächsten Tag hielten sich FOA bedeckt und erläuterten ihre Überlegungen zu Wegen und Erreichbarkeiten. Erst am letzten Tag des Workshops, bei der Präsentation der endgültigen Entwürfe, sollten die jungen Architekten aus London schließlich zeigen, wie sie sich ihr Shoppingcenter vorstellten. Doch die Bauherren mussten sich noch etwas gedulden: FOA waren die Letzten auf der Liste der Vortragenden.

One idea above all was to be included in the architects' deliberations: Could the individual parts of the building not be grouped around a central square – a sort of market place as a focal point, a linking element with fountains, trees and shrubs? A public space could be created here, useful for relaxing coffee breaks and sport, for markets and events. From this square, the thinking continued, there could also be, for example, access to an underground car park. That the desired criteria were entirely realistic had already been proved by the architects of METRO Group Asset Management themselves. Months before the workshop, they had worked out a design. The cinema as a landmark, as well as the position of the individual retail areas, were shown here as well as the links between the building complex with the surrounding city.

Apart from this model, to help the visiting architects in their work, a guided tour was arranged of three selected Istanbul shopping centres – Metro City, Akmerkez and, in the immediate vicinity, the Carrefour – as well as the site on which building was to be situated. Each team was given its own salon in the hotel's business area, all the necessary materials as well as the technical requirements for a direct line to colleagues in their offices in London, Hamburg, Frankfurt and Istanbul.

As early as the evening of the second day the architects were asked to present their initial concepts. The BRT team for example showed how they had at first taken up the client's ideas and envisaged a central square around which all other parts of the building would be arranged. The JSK architects, on the other hand, at the start preferred a modular structure. Instead of one or several larger buildings, they envisaged several small ones, which would partly link together into a larger one. This detailed structure was intended as an allusion to the fragmentary building development of the area immediately surrounding the site. Both Chapman Taylor and Tabanlioğlu made sketches of their preliminary ideas on the building structure. Only FOA, exceptionally and surprisingly, instead of a building merely recorded an analysis of all the route connections. Of a shopping centre there was no sign. At the second presentation next day, FOA again kept a low profile and clarified their thoughts on routes and accessibility. Only on the last day of the workshop, at the presentation of the final designs, did the young architects from London finally show how they envisaged their shopping centre. But the clients had to be patient: FOA were the last on the list of firms making their presentation.

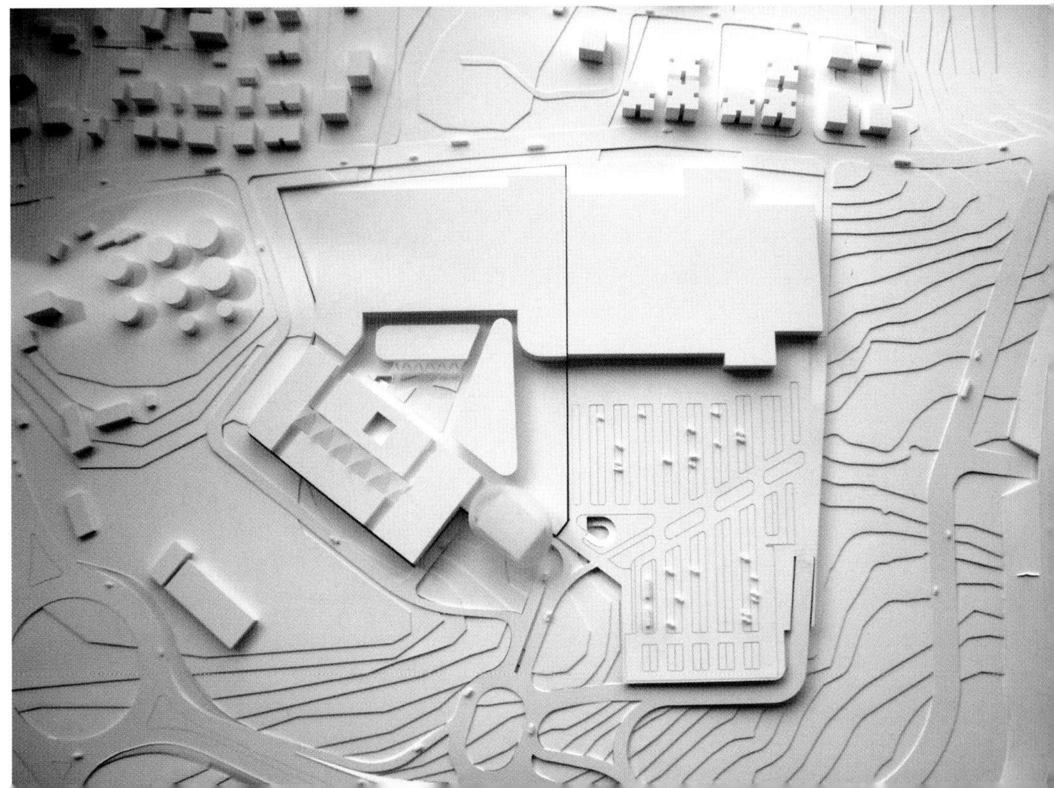

Das Modell der METRO Group Asset Management: Die Gebäude, die sich links an das Möbelhaus Ikea und dessen Parkplatz anfügen, werden um einen zentralen Platz gruppiert.
METRO Group Asset Management model: The buildings, which connect to the Ikea furniture store and its car park on the left, are grouped around a central square.

Ümraniye Terraces von BRT: Schnitt durch die Stockwerke (oben), Blick auf
das Dach mit den Schirmen (Mitte) und auf den gesamten Komplex (unten)
Ümraniye Terraces by BRT: Section through the levels (above), view onto
the roof with umbrellas (centre) and onto the whole complex (below)

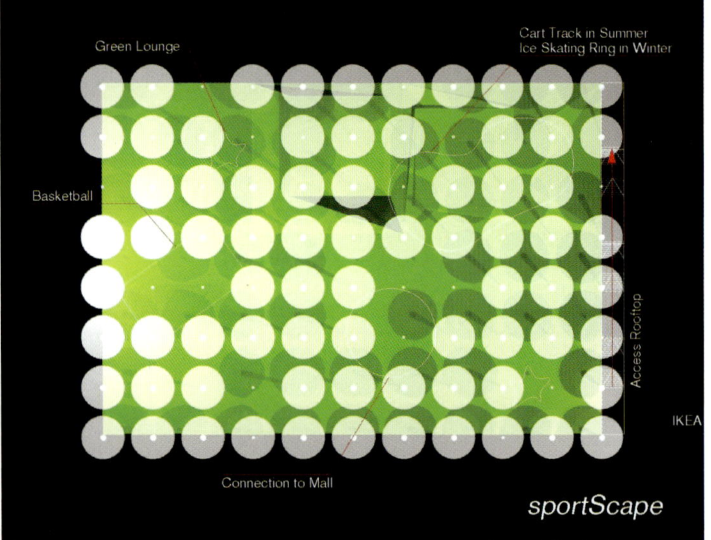

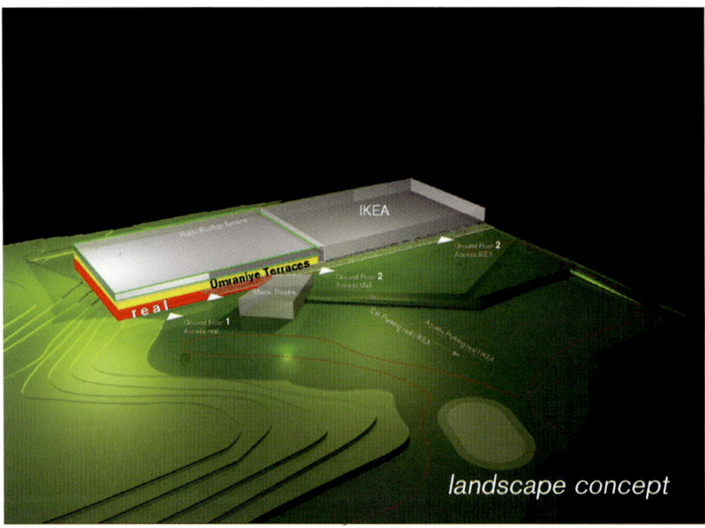

Zuvor zeigten BRT Architekten aus Hamburg ihren Entwurf. „Ümraniye Terraces" haben sie ihn genannt. Von dem Platz zu ebener Erde, den sie noch bei der ersten Ideenpräsentation präferierten, hatten sie sich schnell verabschiedet und ihn kurzerhand auf ihr Gebäude obenauf gelegt. Dieses schließt direkt an Ikea an – und verlängert dessen Korpus in gleicher Breite und Höhe. Im unteren Stockwerk, das tiefer liegt als das Erdgeschoss von Ikea, sollte der Real-Markt einziehen und ein Viertel der Fläche für Parkplätze genutzt werden. In dem Stockwerk darüber befindet sich die Mall. Sie nimmt die gesamte Fläche ein und ist aufgeteilt in die Bereiche „Music", „Fashion" und „Food". An der Vorderseite des Gebäudes bekommt die Mall eine große Terrasse, auf der die Kunden im Freien flanieren können – vor den Winden von einer halbtransparenten Glasscheibe geschützt. Auf dem begrünten Dach darüber kann man im Sommer Basketball spielen, im Winter Schlittschuh laufen. Es gibt eine „Green Lounge" und einen kleinen Teich. Vor der Sonne schützen trichterförmige Schirme, deren strenge schachbrettartige Anordnung auf der Fläche zum Teil unterbrochen wird – für Spielfelder und Sonnenflecken – und deren runde Form sich übrigens in der Fassade wiederfindet: Hier reihen sich weiße Kreise aneinander. Das Kino steht als eigenständiges Gebäude vor dem gesamten Ikea-Mall-Komplex.

Earlier, BRT Architekten from Hamburg presented their design, which they called Ümraniye Terraces. They had swiftly moved on from the idea of the square at ground level, which had been their preference at the first presentation of ideas, and had without further ado placed it on top of their building. This is immediately adjacent to IKEA, and extends its area at the same width and height. On the lower floor, which lies deeper than IKEA's ground floor, they planned to situate the Real hypermarket, a quarter of the space being used for parking. The mall is on the floor above. It takes up the entire area and is divided into three sections, 'Music', 'Fashion' and 'Food'. At the front of the building the mall is given a large terrace, where customers can stroll in the open air, protected from the winds by a semi-transparent glass panel. The grassed roof above can be used for playing basketball in the summer or ice skating in winter. There is a 'Green Lounge' and a small pool. Protection from the sun is given by funnel-shaped umbrellas, whose strict chessboard-like arrangement in the area is partially interrupted by sports fields and sunspots, and whose circular form is incidentally echoed in the façade, where white circles are placed in lines. The cinema is a free-standing building in front of the whole IKEA mall complex.

Der Park auf dem Dach, eine Mall hinter Glas und das Kino als eigenständiges Gebäude – der Entwurf von BRT
The park on the roof, a glazed mall and the cinema as an independent building volume – design by BRT

Variante 1: Dach in Glockenform mit dem offenen
Platz in dessen Mitte (Abbildungen oben).
Variante 2: Parallel zu den hinteren Geschäften
entsteht ein weiterer Gebäudeteil, eine „Shopping
Mall für die Jugend" (Abbildung links).
Alternative 1: bell-shaped roof with an open
square in the centre (above).
Alternative 2: A further building volume is placed
parallel to the rear shops, a "shopping mall for the
youth" (left).

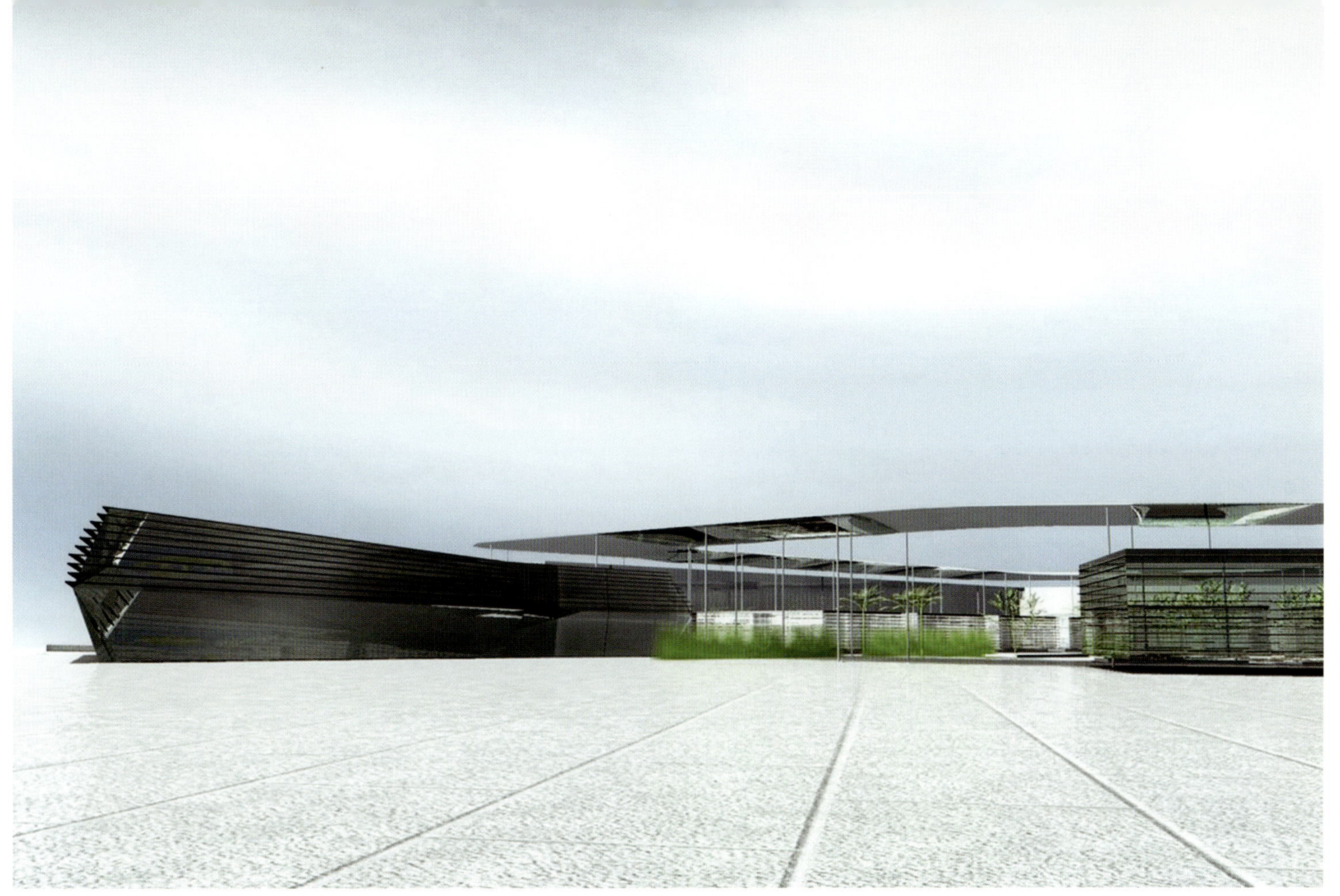

Das Kino als Blickfang – der Entwurf von JSK Architekten, vom Parkplatz aus gesehen
The cinema as an eye catcher – design by JSK Architekten, as seen from the car park

Auch die Ausgangsidee von JSK Architekten wurde im Laufe des Workshops stark modifiziert. Die einzelnen kleinen Baukörper des modularen Systems wuchsen zu größeren Einheiten zusammen. Am Ende stehen sich ein großer Gebäudeteil, der an Ikea in etwa in Ausmaß und Form direkt anschließt, und einige kleinere Gebäude gegenüber. In der Mitte des Komplexes liegt ein natürlich gehaltener Platz mit Bäumen und einem großen Teich, über den kleine Fußgängerbrücken gespannt sind. Die Gebäudeteile haben an ihrer dem Platz zugewandten Seite ein überstehendes Dach, sodass die Passanten in unmittelbarer Nähe der Geschäfte vor Sonne und Regen geschützt flanieren können. Die Mitte des Platzes ist nicht überdacht. In der ersten Variante, welche die Architekten vorlegten, ähnelt die Dachkonstruktion und die Anordnung der Gebäude von oben betrachtet dem Umriss einer Glocke. In einer zweiten Variante wird diese Symmetrie aufgebrochen. Das Dach wird hinter die kleinteilige Ladenzeile gezogen und teilweise zu einer Art Rampe, sodass parallel zu den Geschäften ein weiterer Gebäudeteil – „Shoppingmall für die Jugend" – entsteht. „Die Architektur reagiert auf ihre Nutzung", erklären die Architekten, „wo sie hoch sein muss, ist sie erhöht, wo sie niedrig sein soll, senkt sie sich."

The initial ideas of JSK Architekten were also greatly modified in the course of the workshop. The small individual structures of the modular system grew into larger units. Finally, a large building, comparable to IKEA in dimensions and form, and several smaller ones are placed opposite each other. In the centre of the complex is a square, kept in a natural state with trees and a large pond, spanned by small footbridges. On the side facing the square, the buildings have an overhanging roof, so that passers-by strolling in the immediate vicinity of the stores are protected from sun and rain. The centre of the square is not covered. In the first version presented by the architects, the roof construction and the arrangement of the buildings, seen from above, resembles the outline of a bell. In a second version, this symmetry is broken up. The roof is taken back behind the row of individual shops and partly becomes a kind of ramp, so that parallel to the shops a further part of the building evolves called 'Shopping Mall for Youth'. "The architecture reacts to its use," the architects explain. "Where it needs to be high, it is raised, and where it needs to be low, it is lowered."

Das Shoppingcenter von Chapman Taylor besteht aus verschiedenen Gebäuden, die durch ein langes, geschwungenes Dach miteinander verbunden werden. Wie ein spiegelverkehrtes S sieht diese Struktur aus der Vogelperspektive aus, deren oberer Bogen sich nahtlos an das Möbelhaus anschließt: Im Erdgeschoss befindet sich der Real-Markt, darüber, auf einem begrünten Dach, ein Sportplatz. Im zweiten Bogen ist die eigentliche Mall, an die sich ein glasüberdachter Arkadengang und – in der Mitte des Bogens – ein weiterer Shop-Komplex anschließen. Ein typisches Shoppingcenter erwartet den Besucher hier. Vor den Eingängen zu den Arkaden wird ein kleiner Platz geschaffen, der von einem spitzen Turm flankiert wird. Und dort, wo das S aufhört, spaltet sich das schlangenförmige Dach. Die beiden Enden umschließen das zweigeschossige Kinogebäude, das vom Parkplatz aus den Eingang zur Mall markiert.

Chapman Taylor's shopping centre consists of various buildings, linked together by a long, curved roof. From a bird's-eye perspective this structure looks like a mirror-image of a letter S, whose upper curve seamlessly adjoins the furniture store. The Real hypermarket is on the ground floor, and a sports field is above, on a grassed roof. The actual mall is in the second curve, adjoining a glass-roofed arcade and, in the centre of the curve, a further complex of shops. Here a typical shopping centre awaits the visitor. A small square is created in front of the entrance to the arcades, flanked by a pointed tower. And where the letter S ends, the snake-shaped roof divides. The two ends surround the two-storey cinema building, which from the car park marks the entrance to the mall.

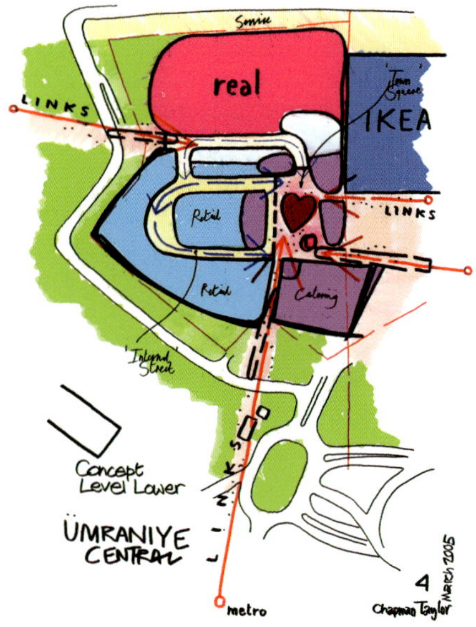

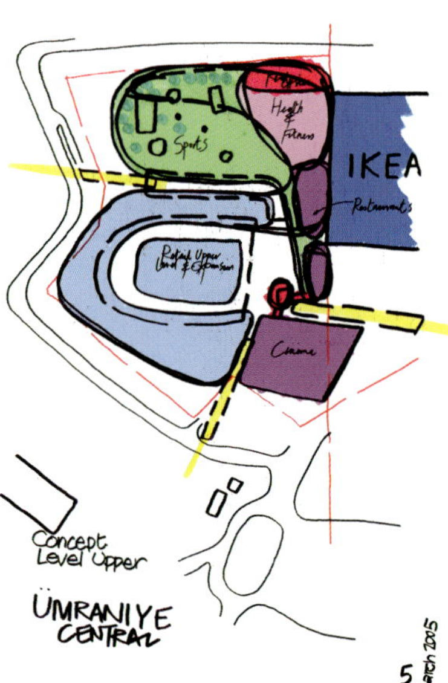

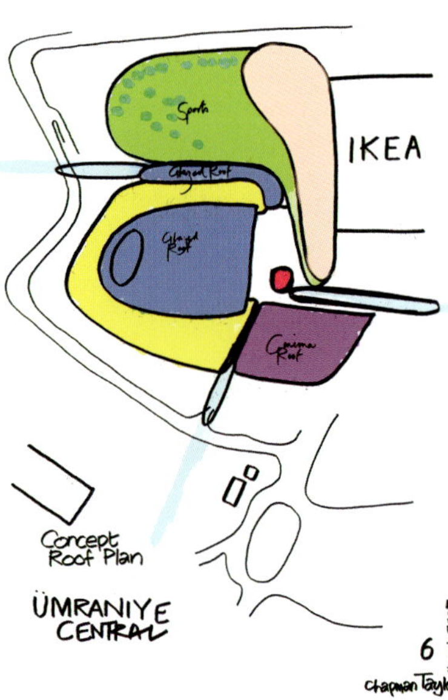

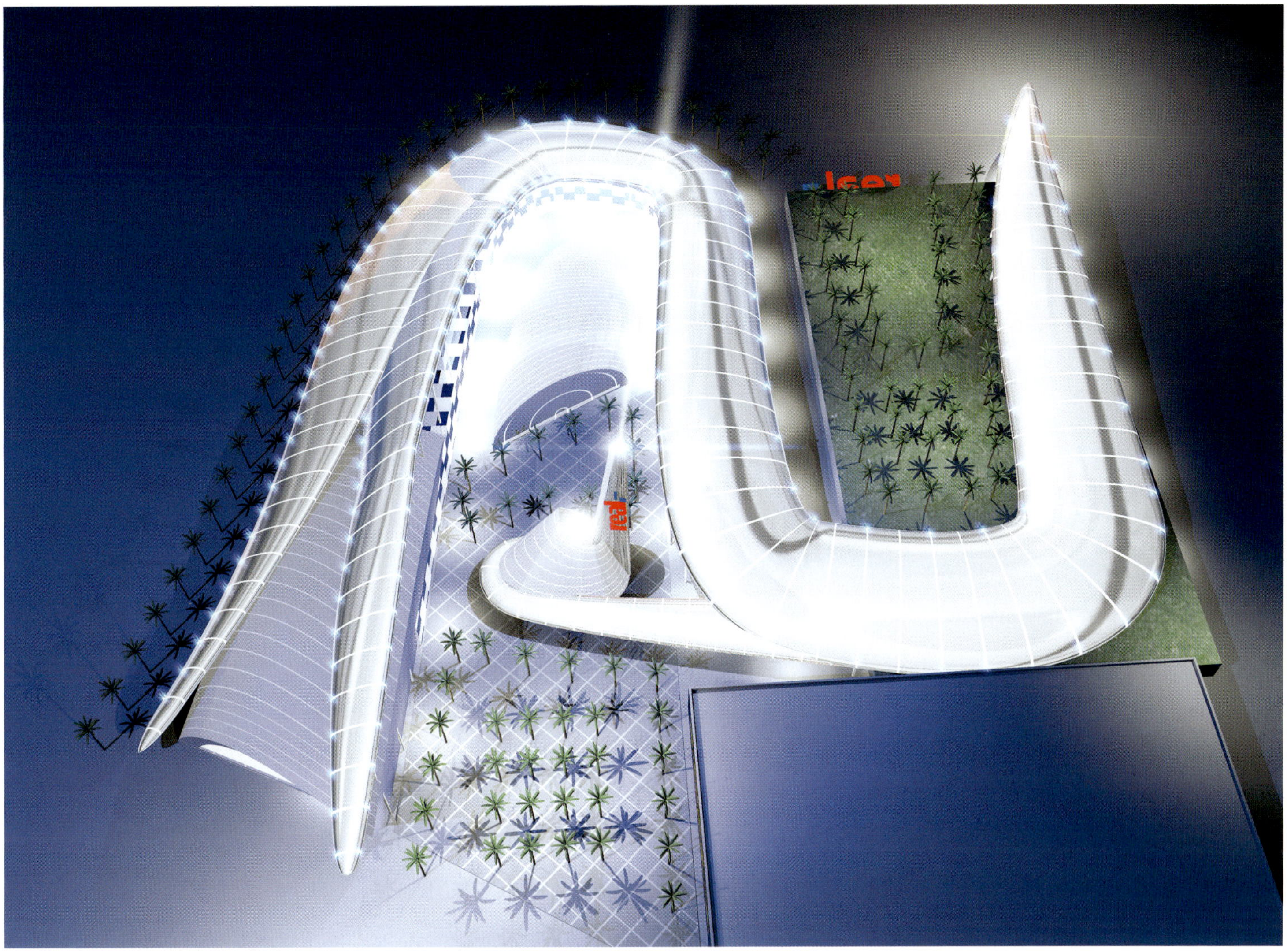

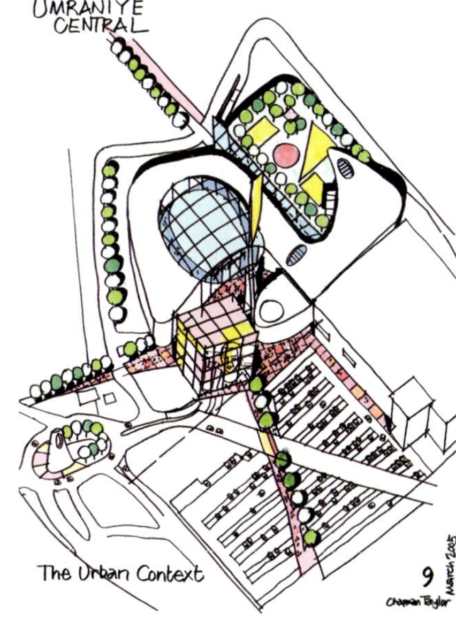

Shoppingcenter in Schlangenform: Der Entwurf von Chapman Taylor aus der Vogelperspektive (oben). Skizzen der verschiedenen Stockwerke vom Erdgeschoss bis zum Dach (unten links) und vom gesamten Komplex in seinem Kontext (unten rechts)

Snake-shaped shopping centre: Bird's eye view of design by Chapman Taylor (above). Sketches of the various levels from the ground floor to the roof (below left) and of the whole complex and its environs (below right).

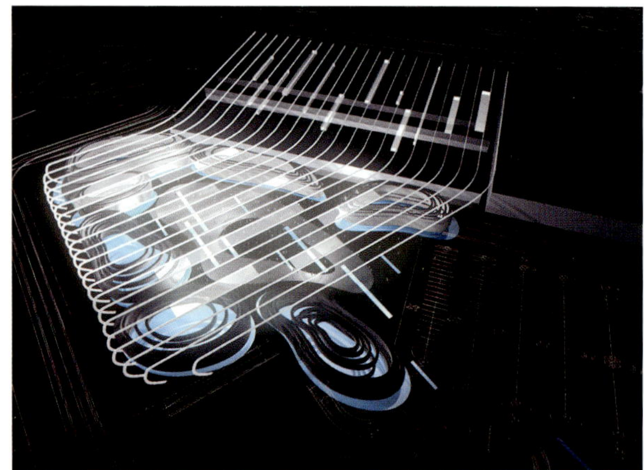

Shoppingcenter mit Schiebedach: Der gesamte Komplex wird von einem Dach überspannt (Abbildungen rechts oben und links), darunter gruppieren sich die Themenwelten in eigenen Gebäudeteilen (rechts unten).
Shopping centre with sliding roof: One roof covers the whole complex (above right and left), different theme areas are organised into individual building volumes below (below right).

Auch beim Entwurf von Tabanlioğlu verbindet ein gemeinsames Dach verschiedene Gebäude – nur dass hier das gesamte Areal überspannt wird und sich das Dach in der Mitte, über einer Plaza, öffnen lässt. Ähnlich wie bei den Entwürfen von JSK und BRT schließt sich zunächst an Ikea ein großes Gebäude an – mit Real im Erdgeschoss und einer „Active Area" auf dem Dach. Auch hier wird das Dach für einen Sportplatz genutzt, es gibt eine Joggingbahn, eine Anlage für Mini-Golf, eine Kletterwand und in der Mitte des Dachs einen Swimmingpool. Doch auch auf der geplanten Plaza kann Sport getrieben werden. An bestimmten „Sport Days" soll der Platz, auf dem die Kunden sonst Kaffee trinken und Kinder spielen, auch dafür genutzt werden. An den Seiten der Plaza stehen Gebäude in unterschiedlicher Form und Größe, die jeweils Shops zu einem bestimmten Thema – Casual World, Electronic, ein Kaufhaus und Sport – beherbergen. Wie verzauberte Findlinge liegen sie da.

The Tabanlioğlu design too links different buildings with a common roof – only here the entire area is spanned and the roof is open in the middle, over a plaza. As with the JSK and BRT designs, a large building is adjacent to IKEA, with Real on the ground floor and an 'Active Area' on the roof. Here too the roof is used as a sports area, with a jogging track, a mini-golf course, a climbing wall and in the centre of the roof a swimming pool. But sports can also be played on the planned plaza. On certain 'Sport Days' this square, where at other times customers can drink coffee and children play, can also be used for this purpose. Along the sides of the plaza stand buildings of various shapes and sizes, which each accommodate shops on a specific theme – Casual World, Electronic, a department store and Sport. They stand in the plaza like enchanted erratic boulders in a landscape.

IKEA
SPORTS ACTIVITY AREA
HEALTH CLUB
REAL
CINEMAS
MALL
MALL
MALL
MALL
MALL
MALL
MALL
THEME PLAZA
FOUR SEASON ACTIVITY

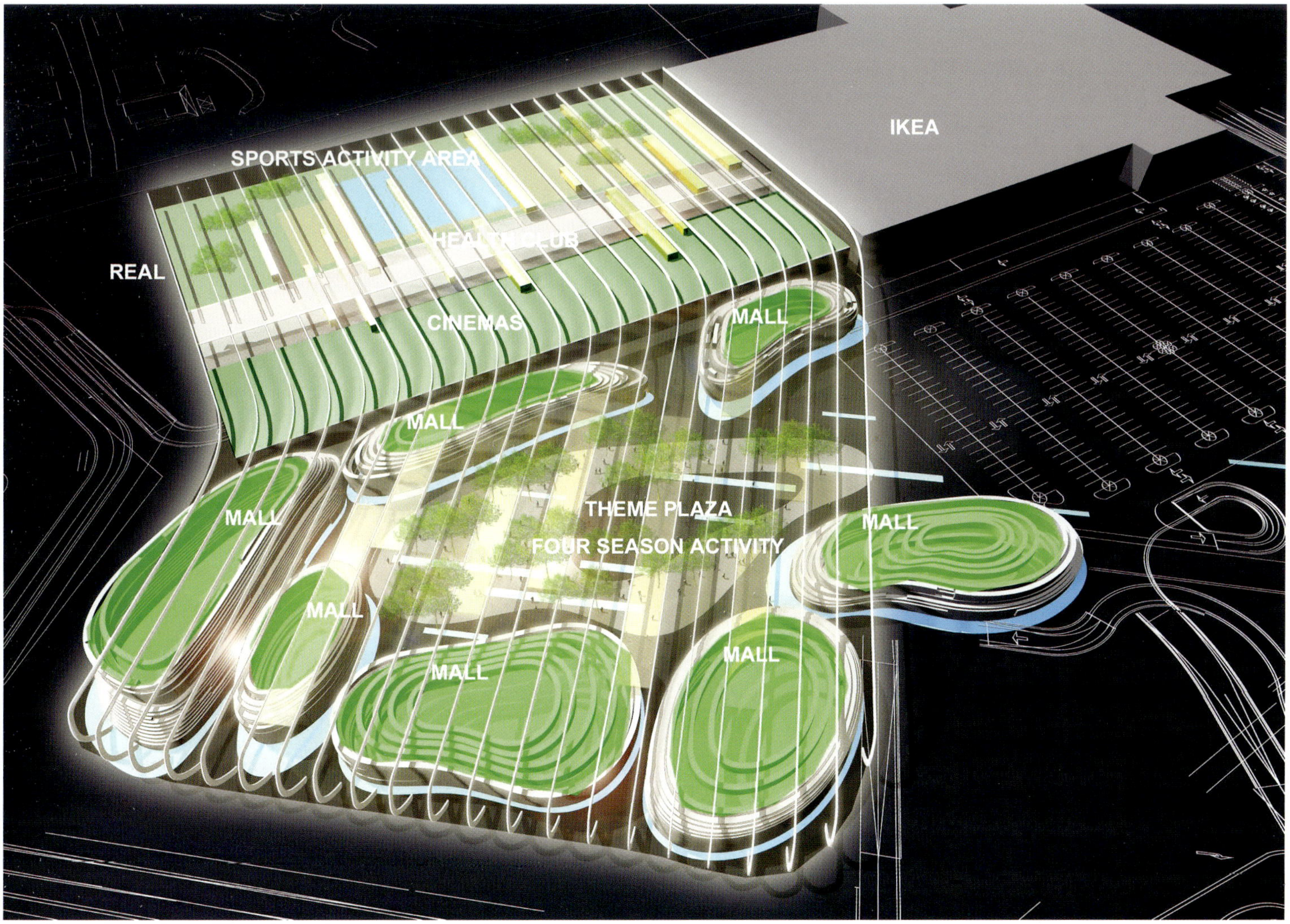

Die Präsentation von FOA beginnt mit einer Kritik am Status quo: „Architects sometimes like to believe that there is one ideal solution for every challenge" – Architekten glauben gern, dass es eine einzige ideale Lösung gibt, die auf jede erdenkliche Herausforderung passt. FOA hingegen, so machen sie schnell klar, gehen davon aus, dass es statt einer einzigen verschiedene prototypische Lösungen gibt, deren Erfolg in ihrer Fähigkeit liegt, sich ständig anzupassen – „we would like to think that there are prototypical solutions, whose success is their ability to adapt consistently". Schneeflocken illustrieren, was gemeint ist: Keine gleicht der anderen, aber alle sind ähnlich in der Struktur – spezifische Variationen eines Systems.
Der Prototyp einer Mall, den die Architekten als Nächstes skizzieren, ist keine Schneeflocke: „Big and beautiful" steht er auf ebenem Grund – mit einem gewaltigen Parkplatz vor der Tür. Es ist das typische Shoppingcenter, das man von den grünen Wiesen kennt. Eine einzige Größe muss für alle möglichen Situationen passen: für Tage und Tageszeiten, an denen wenig Besucher kommen, ebenso wie in Stoßzeiten. Wachstum heißt Wiederholung des ewig gleichen Systems: Variationen, Verkleinerung oder Wandel sind nicht möglich.

FOA's presentation begins with a critique of the status quo: "Architects sometimes like to believe that there is one ideal solution for every challenge." FOA on the other hand, as they swiftly make clear, start from the principle that instead of one, "there are prototypical solutions, whose success is their ability to adapt consistently." Snowflakes illustrate their meaning: no two are the same, but all have a similar structure – they are specific variations on a system.
The prototype of a mall which is next sketched out by the architects is no snowflake. 'Big and beautiful', it stands on level ground, with a huge car park by the door. It is the typical greenfield site shopping centre. One size must fit all possible situations: for days and times of day when few visitors come, as well as peak periods. Growth means repetition of the eternally similar system: variation, reduction and change are not possible.

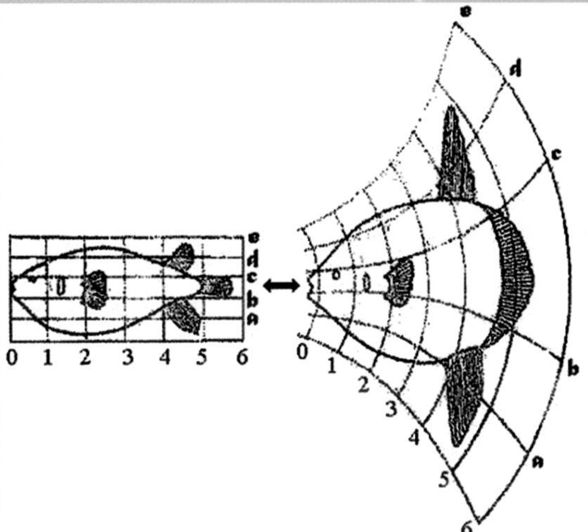

Aus der Präsentation von FOA: Eine ideale Lösung für alle Probleme (links)
versus prototypische Lösungen, die sich an unterschiedliche Gegebenheiten
anpassen können (rechts)
From the presentation by FOA: An ideal solution for all of the problems (left)
versus prototypical solutions which can adapt to varying circumstances (right)

Neue Prototypen müssen also entwickelt werden, die flexibler sind und sich den Gegebenheiten anpassen können. Was man dazu braucht, haben FOA in Form einer Einkaufsliste zusammengestellt. Ganz oben stehen „Circulation and Power". Am Beispiel der „Frankfurter Küche" der österreichischen Architektin Margarete Schütte Lihotzky aus dem Jahr 1926 wird erklärt, wie man Wege und Aufenthaltszeiten optimieren kann: So wurde hier zum Beispiel, nach gründlichem Studium der zurückzulegenden Schritte einer Hausfrau, die durchschnittliche Entfernung von Herd zu Esstisch mehr als halbiert. Und mit Blick auf die historischen Stadtpläne von Kassel und Berlin stellen die Architekten zweierlei fest: Zum einen müssen die Größenverhältnisse im Raum variieren. Zum anderen bedarf es Beschränkungen, um Dichte zu erreichen. Für die prototypischen Shoppingcenter heißt das zunächst, dass der große Parkplatz vor den Türen weichen muss und stattdessen kleinere, individuell zugängliche Parkplätze geschaffen werden. Der dadurch frei gewordene Platz vor der Tür wird nun für den Einzelhandel genutzt – zu ebener Erde wie auch auf verschiedenen Etagen. Wie diese Fläche gestaltet wird, macht der zweite Punkt auf der Liste deutlich: „Identity and Branding". Die Gebäude werden unterteilt, aufgefächert und mit Zwischenräumen aufgelockert. Das Vorbild dafür haben FOA als Fotografie dabei: Es sind die italienischen Piazze mittelalterlicher Städte wie Siena. Unter „Growth and Change of Use" wird schließlich gezeigt, wie sich das bis dato entwickelte Modell – bestehend aus dem großen Baukörper und der thematisch untergliederten Shopzeile davor – erweitern lässt. Immer größer könnten die Themenbereiche werden und immer unabhängiger von dem im Vergleich dazu eher statischen Hauptgebäude, bis sie in den urbanen Kontext eindringen und Blöcke, Straßen und Muster bilden.

New prototypes must therefore be developed which are more flexible and adaptable to different conditions. FOA have drawn up a shopping list for what is needed. Right at the top of the list is 'Circulation and Power'. Using the example of the 'Frankfurt Kitchen' of 1926 by the Austrian architect Margarete Schütte Lihotzky, they explain how routes and length of stay can be optimized. For example, a systematic study of the steps taken by a housewife shows how the average distance from oven to dining table can be reduced by more than half. And with a look at the historic city maps of Kassel and Berlin the architects come to two conclusions: For one thing, the relationships of size must vary in the space. For another, restrictions are needed to achieve density. For the prototypical shopping centre, this means for a start that the huge car park in front of the doors must be eliminated, and instead smaller, individually accessible car parks must be created. The space in front of the doors that thus becomes vacant will now be used for retail trade outlets – on the ground floor as well as on different floors. How this area will be used is made clear by the second point on the list: 'Identity and Branding'. The buildings are subdivided, separately developed and loosened up by intermediate spaces. FOA produced a model for this in photographic form: the Italian piazzas of medieval towns such as Siena. Finally, under 'Growth and Change of Use' it is shown how the model developed to date – consisting of the large building corpus and the thematically subdivided rows of shops in front – can be extended. The themed areas could become ever larger and ever more independent from the comparatively rather static main building, until they penetrate into the urban context and form blocks, streets and patterns.

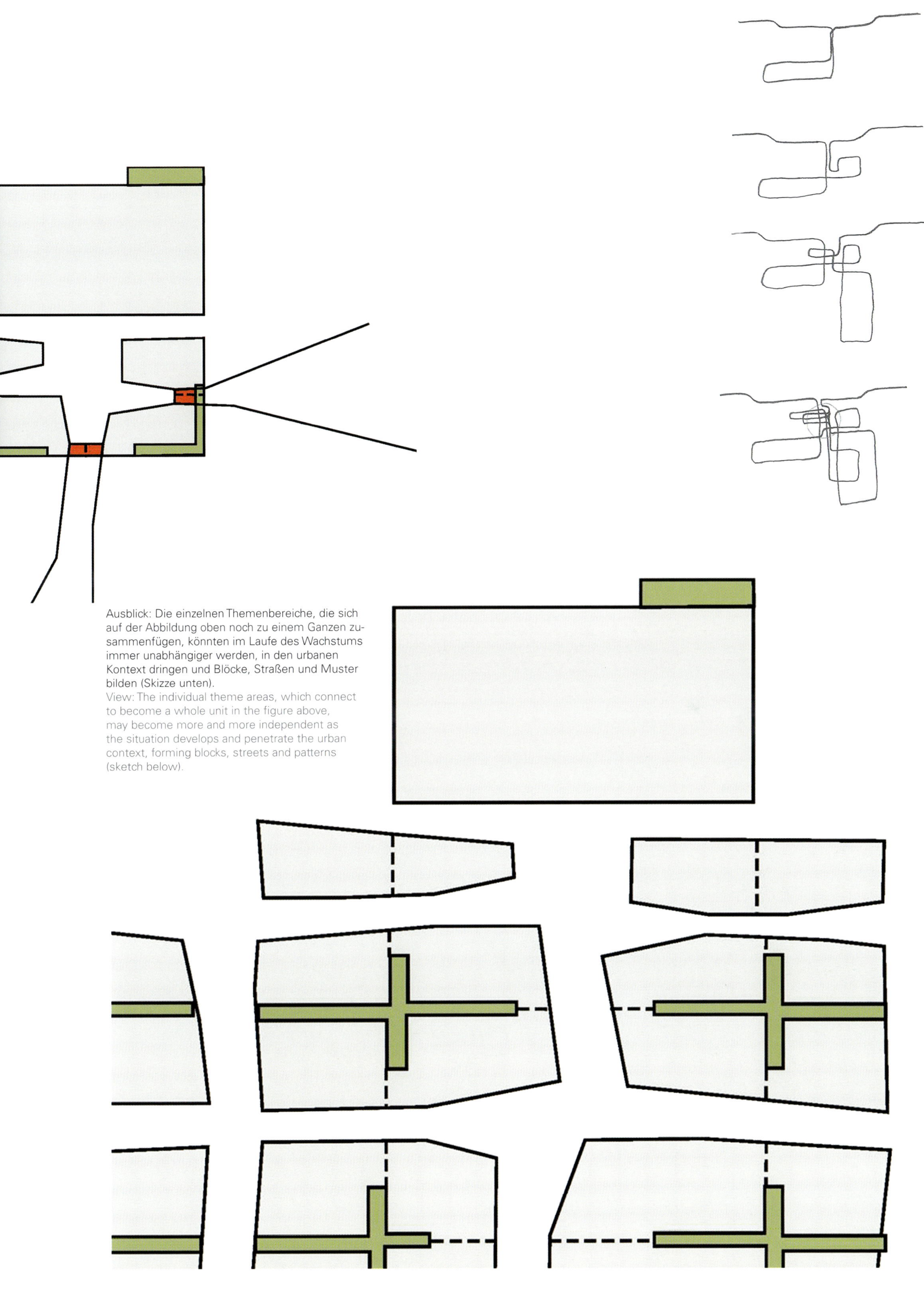

Ausblick: Die einzelnen Themenbereiche, die sich auf der Abbildung oben noch zu einem Ganzen zusammenfügen, könnten im Laufe des Wachstums immer unabhängiger werden, in den urbanen Kontext dringen und Blöcke, Straßen und Muster bilden (Skizze unten).
View: The individual theme areas, which connect to become a whole unit in the figure above, may become more and more independent as the situation develops and penetrate the urban context, forming blocks, streets and patterns (sketch below).

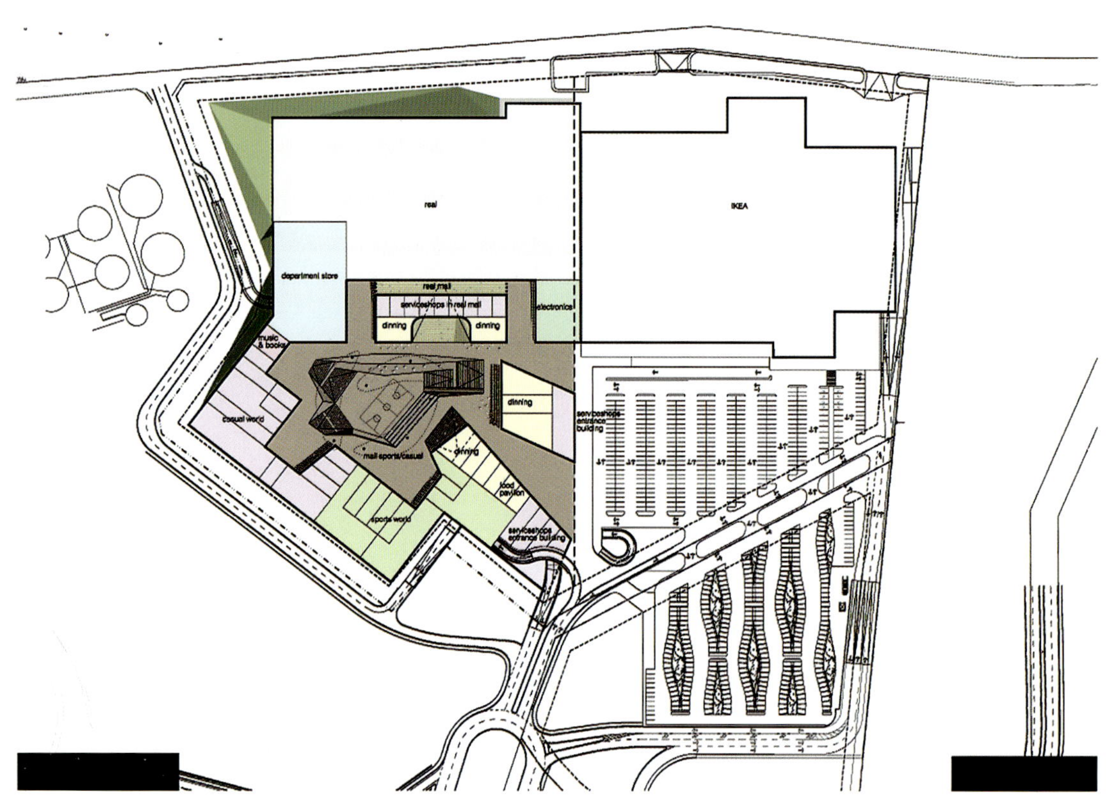

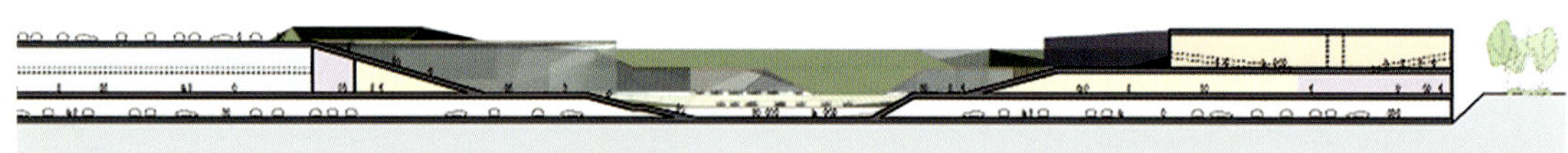

Schnitt durch den Shopping
Square von FOA
Section through the shopping
square by FOA

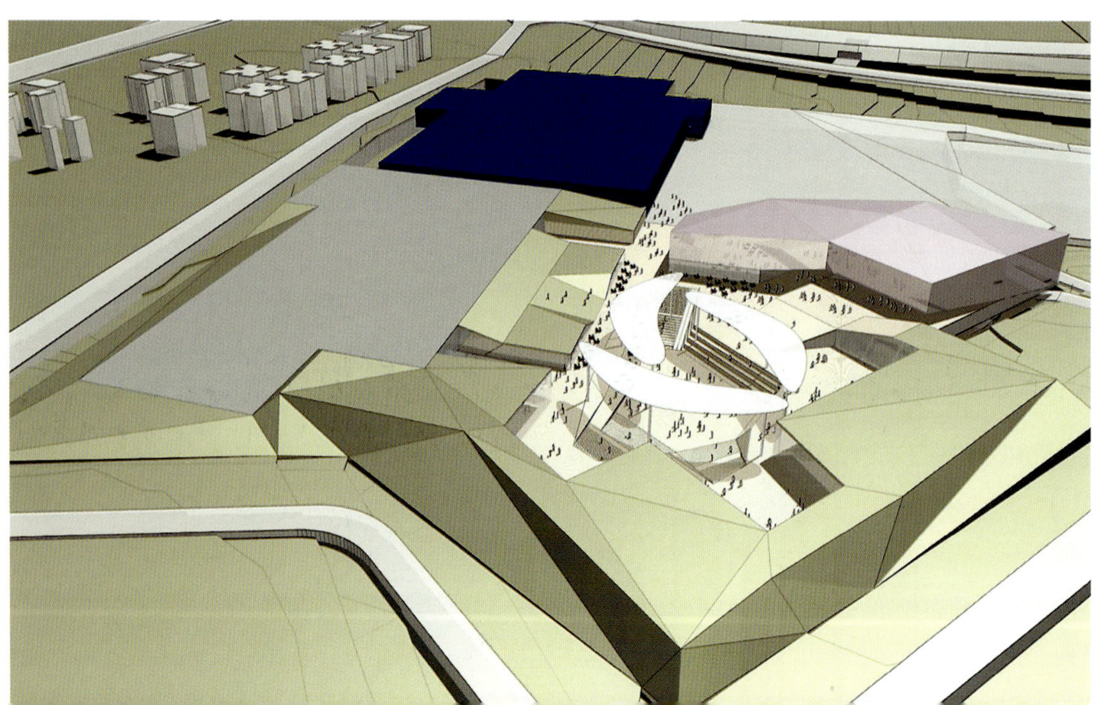

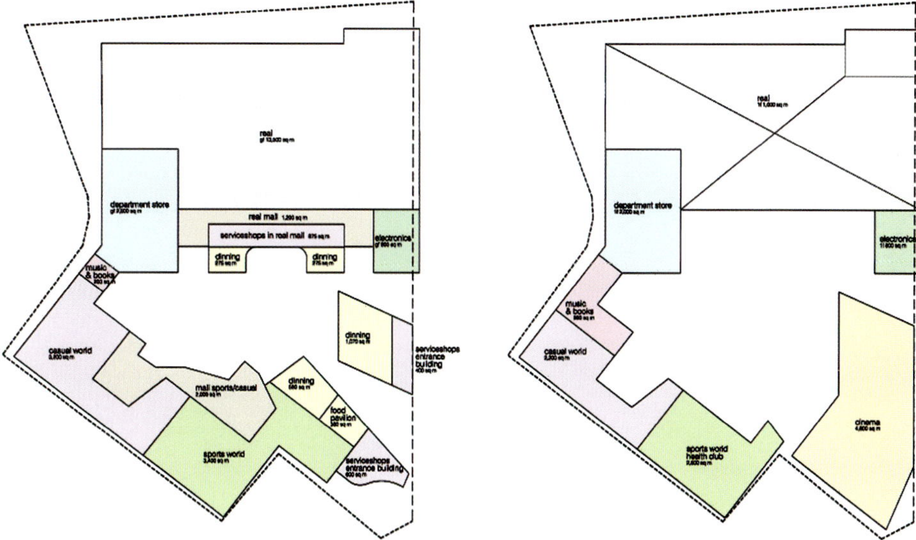

Erst im dritten Teil der Präsentation werden FOA schließlich konkret und zeigen ihre Variante eines passenden Prototyps für das entsprechende Grundstück: Auch in ihrem Entwurf schließt ein quadratischer Bau direkt an Ikea an. Davor öffnet sich der Raum zu einem öffentlichen Platz, um den sich die einzelnen Themenbereiche aneinanderfügen: Media World, Casual World, Sports World, Food im Erdgeschoss, darüber ein Fitnessclub über den Sportgeschäften, die Kino World über der Gastronomie. Die Architektur wirkt gleichsam wie aus dem Boden gefaltet, es gibt Rampen und Treppen, die in der Mitte auf einen etwas vertieft gelegenen, großzügigen Platz führen. Die Dächer sind begehbar und das Center somit aus allen vorhandenen Richtungen in den städtischen Kontext eingebunden.

Bei näherer Betrachtung fällt auf, dass FOA sehr nahe am ursprünglichen Konzept der METRO Group Asset Management geblieben sind, dieses aber auf außergewöhnliche Weise transformiert und verfeinert haben. Die Dynamik der miteinander verschmolzenen Baukörper, die konsequente Ausrichtung an den geforderten Grundprinzipien, die Einbettung in den landschaftlichen Kontext sowie die unkonventionelle Auseinandersetzung in der Entwicklung eines Prototypen machen den Entwurf von FOA unverwechselbar und bestechend logisch.

Nach der Präsentation von FOA stand der Sieger für viele der Teilnehmer schon fest. Doch die Mitarbeiter von METRO Group Asset Management nahmen sich noch ein wenig Zeit. Zurück in Düsseldorf, verglichen sie die Modelle genau, prüften, welches ihren Vorstellungen am nächsten kam, und entschieden sich schließlich für: FOA.

Not until they come to the third part of their presentation do FOA finally become specific, showing their variations on an appropriate prototype for the site in question. In their design too a square building directly adjoins IKEA. In front of it, the space is opened out to a public square, around which the individually themed areas cluster: Media World, Casual World, Sports World, Food on the ground floor, above them a fitness centre above the sports shops, a cinema above the food shops. The architecture seems to develop out of the ground, there are ramps and staircases, which lead in the centre to a slightly sunken, imposing square. The roofs are accessible and the centre is thus linked to its urban context in all available directions.

On closer examination it is striking that FOA have kept very closely to METRO Group Asset Management's original concept, but have transformed and refined it in an exceptional way. The dynamics of the merging building structures, the consistent arrangement according to the basic principles stipulated, the embedding in the local context as well as the unconventional approach to the development of a prototype make FOA's design unmistakably and irresistibly logical.

After FOA's presentation, many of the participants were in no doubt as to the winner. But the METRO Group Asset Management staff took a little longer to make their decision. Back in Düsseldorf they carefully compared the models, considered which of them came closest to their ideas, and finally decided in favour of FOA.

FOREIGN OFFICE ARCHITECTS: EIN GESPRÄCH
A CONVERSATION

London, Stadtteil Hackney, Curtain Road 55. Man läuft fast daran vorbei. Kein Schild, das weithin sichtbar auf das Architekturbüro hinweist, keine durchgestylte Rezeption, die den Gast empfängt. Stattdessen fühlt sich, wer die unscheinbare Glastür gefunden hat, ein bisschen wie in einer jener Galerien, die in angesagten Großstadtvierteln gerade durch ihre reduzierte, unaufdringliche Gestaltung auffallen. Und tatsächlich hat er etwas von einer Galerie, der Eingangsbereich zu den Büros von FOA: In dem Raum stehen die Modelle, welche die Architekten in den letzten Jahren entwarfen und die für so großes Aufsehen sorgten, dass Museen sie anforderten, um sie zu präsentieren. Was von den Ausstellungen wieder zurückkam, wurde im Untergeschoss des Gebäudes abgestellt und fügt sich so, eher zufällig und kaum arrangiert, zu einer spontanen Retrospektive des bisherigen Wirkens von FOA zusammen.

Wie verdrehte Schläuche schrauben sich da die Bundled Towers in die Höhe – ein Prototyp für eine neue Art Wolkenkratzer, entworfen in Zusammenhang mit dem Wettbewerbsbeitrag für Ground Zero in New York. Die BBC Music Box für London ist als Modell zu sehen, welche die sonst vor der Öffentlichkeit versteckten Studios zur Bühne machen: Nur eine Glasmembran trennt die Musiker von dem zufälligen

FOAs Vorschlag für Ground Zero in New York: die Bundled Towers
FOA's proposal for Ground Zero, New York City: the Bundled Towers

London, 55 Curtain Road, Hackney. One almost walks past it. No prominent sign to alert one from afar to the location of the architectural office, no stylish reception area to welcome the visitor. Instead, anyone who has found the unpretentious glass door feels a little as though in one of those galleries in trendy urban districts which impress precisely because of their minimal, unobtrusive design. And in fact the entrance area to the FOA offices does have something of the gallery about it. In this space stand the models designed by the architects in recent years, which caused such a sensation that museums requested to be allowed to display them. Whatever came back from the exhibitions was stored in the basement of the building and thus forms, rather accidentally and hardly arranged in any order, a spontaneous retrospective of FOA's work to date.

Like distorted hosepipes, the Bundled Towers spiral upwards – a prototype for a new kind of skyscraper, designed in connection with the competition entry for Ground Zero in New York. The BBC Music Box for London is to be seen here in model form, making the studios, otherwise hidden from public view, into a stage; only a glass membrane separates the musicians from chance passers-by in the street. Then there is the Institute of Legal Medicine for Madrid in miniature, slightly suggestive of a glass doughnut. And, not to be forgotten, the prizewinning Yokohama Project – the ferry terminal for cruise ships near Tokyo, whose fascination lies less in a clearly outlined architecture than in the manner in which the building is integrated into

Publikum auf der Straße. Dann gibt es das Institute of Legal Medicine für Madrid im Kleinformat, das ein bisschen an einen gläsernen Donut erinnert. Und nicht fehlen darf natürlich das preisgekrönte Yokohama Project – der Fähranleger für Kreuzfahrtschiffe vor Tokio, dessen Faszination weniger in einer klar umrissenen Architektur liegt als vielmehr in der Art und Weise, wie sich das Gebäude in den umliegenden Kontext integriert. Eins neben dem anderen hocken die Modelle auf ihren großen Transportkisten, so, als warteten sie schon auf ihre nächste Reise. Oder zumindest auf ihren Aufstieg in eine der oberen Etagen.
Aber da ist kaum Platz. Rund 50 Architekten arbeiten im Moment im Londoner Büro, für 40 war die Haushälfte, welche die Gründer Farshid Moussavi und Alejandro Zaera-Polo vor einigen Jahren kauften, nachdem ihr altes Apartment für das wachsende Büro zu klein geworden war, nur ausgelegt. Und so sitzen die ersten Mitarbeiter inzwischen auf der Etage, die eigentlich ausschließlich für Besprechungen vorgesehen war. Grüne Vorhänge trennen den Raum in mehrere Zonen, orangefarbene Stühle, einst entworfen von Charles Eames, gruppieren sich um die gläsernen Tische. Von draußen klingt der Straßenlärm durch die Fenster und hinter dem Vorhang diskutieren die Architekten.

Die meisten Architekturbüros heißen so wie die Architekten, die das Büro gegründet haben. Dieses Büro wiederum nennt sich Foreign Office Architects. Was war die ursprüngliche Programmatik dieses Namens?

Der Begriff Foreigner, Ausländer oder Fremder hat ja oft eine erstmal negative Konnotation: Man steht außen vor, kommt aus dem falschen Land. Diese Position kann aber auch eine der Stärke sein. Man sieht viele Dinge anders, man stellt andere Fragen als die Einheimischen, die vielleicht schon zu sehr an Teile des Status quo gewöhnt sind, als dass sie diesen in Frage stellen würden. Die Situation des Außenstehenden hat daher oft auch Qualitäten und Möglichkeiten, aus denen man kreative Potenziale ziehen kann.

Wie beeinflussen die verschiedenen Backgrounds der Architekten die Arbeit?

Zum einen gibt es da die Erfahrungen und Hintergründe, die jeder von uns mit sich herumträgt, sozusagen als Handgepäck, und zum anderen die spezifischen Bedingungen vor Ort, mit denen wir uns auseinandersetzen müssen und wollen. Das geht nicht ohne Bezug auf unsere mitgebrachten Erfahrungen. Im Gegenteil: Wir finden es sehr spannend, lokale Erfindungen in anderen Kontexten zu testen. Andererseits ist uns der spezifische Ort sehr wichtig, die Lösung, die wir finden, muss aus dem Ort erwachsen und nicht von Außen implantiert werden.

Für einen Architekturwettbewerb war die Methode von METRO Group Asset Management relativ ungewöhnlich: Es wurden fünf Büros nach Istanbul eingeladen, die innerhalb eines Wochenendes ihre eigenen Entwürfe erarbeiten und präsentieren sollten. Wie fanden Sie diese Methode?

the surrounding context. Side by side, the models squat on their large containers as though already awaiting their next journey. Or at least their ascent to one of the upper floors.

But there is hardly room for them there. Some 50 architects currently work in the London office, based in half a building intended for only 40, and bought by the founders, Farshid Moussavi und Alejandro Zaera-Polo, a few years ago when their old apartment had become too small for the growing firm. And so the first staff members are seated on the floor that was actually intended exclusively as a conference area. Green curtains divide the space into several zones; orange-coloured chairs designed by Charles Eames are grouped around the glass tables. From outside, street noises are heard through the window, and behind the curtains the architects are holding a discussion.

Most architectural firms are called after the architects who founded them. But this firm is called Foreign Office Architects. What was the original idea behind this name?

The concept of the foreigner sometimes has an initially negative connotation; you are an outsider, you come from the wrong country. But this position can be one of strength. You see a lot of things differently, you put other questions than those of the local people, who are perhaps already too used to parts of the status quo to challenge them. So the situation of the outsider often has qualities and possibilities from which one can draw creative potential.

How do your different backgrounds influence your work?

On the one hand there are the experiences and backgrounds that each of us carries around, more or less as hand luggage, and on the other hand the specific conditions on site, with which we need and want to come to terms. This can't happen without reference to the experience we have brought along. On the contrary, we find it very exciting to test our local discoveries in other contexts. On the other hand, the specific location is very important to us; the solution we find must grow out of the location and not be implanted from the outside.

For an architectural competition, the method used by METRO Group Asset Management was relatively unusual. Five firms were invited to Istanbul to work out and present their own designs in the space of a weekend. What did you think of this method?

On the one hand very effective; the stakes were relatively low. If you spend only a weekend on a design, you can get over it more easily if you are not the winner of the race. With a normal architectural competition, as a rule one loses much more time. And of course it is all the more gratifying if you win a competition after only a weekend's work. On the other hand, in such a short time you can only speculate about a number of details and questions; You have to make a lot of assumptions that can't be proved. And then it is very unusual to organize a competition as a weekend workshop, where everyone has to present on each day what has been worked out since breakfast.

Passanten werden zum Publikum:
Die BBC Music Box für London
Passers-by become spectators: the
BBC Music Box in London

Zum einen sehr effektiv: Die Einsätze sind relativ niedrig. Wer nur ein Wochenende in einen Entwurf steckt, kann es besser verschmerzen, wenn er nicht als Sieger aus dem Rennen hervorgeht. Bei einem normalen Architektenwettbewerb verliert man in der Regel viel mehr Zeit. Und umso erfreulicher natürlich, wenn man an nur einem Wochenende einen Wettbewerb gewinnt. Andererseits kann man in der kurzen Zeit bei vielen Details und Fragen nur spekulieren, man muss viele Annahmen machen, die man nicht prüfen kann. Und dann ist es sehr ungewöhnlich, einen Wettbewerb als Wochenend-Workshop zu veranstalten, wo jeder täglich präsentiert, was er seit dem Frühstück so entwickelt hat.

Wie haben die eingeladenen Büros vor Ort gearbeitet? Wurde die Zeit am Ende für alle nicht sehr knapp?

Alle konkurrierenden Büros aus Deutschland, England und der Türkei waren mit zwei oder drei Teilnehmern angereist, aber in ihren Hauptquartieren hatten sie jeweils ein größeres Team, das ihnen aus der Ferne fleißig zuarbeitete. Das war bei uns nicht so. Wir waren erst zu zweit, dann zu dritt vor Ort, in London waren alle an dem Wochenende mit anderen Deadlines beschäftigt. Wie bei jedem Wettbewerb wird es am Ende natürlich immer ein wenig eng und so haben wir es nicht geschafft, den Kollegen in London die Entwurfspräsentation noch mal zu zeigen, bevor wir präsentierten. Das ist uns aber auch schon so manches Mal in London passiert. Unsere Projekte sind oft über mehrere Kontinente verstreut, und so lernt man, die Entwurfsdiskussionen auch mal mit E-Mail, Telefon und Fax zu führen.

Wie wichtig ist die interne Diskussion, wie wichtig ist es FOA, dass alle Entwürfe eine typische Handschrift erkennen lassen?

Bei FOA gibt es keine feste formale Handschrift und es besteht auch kein Interesse daran, eine so festgelegte Handschrift zu entwickeln. Genauso wenig gibt es einen Genius mit einem Stift, dessen Untergebenen seine Skizzen durchzeichnen müssen. Was es jedoch gibt, ist eine gewisse Art und Weise, Projekte zu verstehen, zu diskutieren und zu recherchieren und aus den Erkenntnissen Entwürfe zu entwickeln und wachsen zu lassen.

Können Sie diese Methode am Beispiel Istanbul erklären? Wie sind Sie dabei vorgegangen?

Wir haben uns zunächst sehr ausführlich mit den grundsätzlichen Problemen auseinandergesetzt, welche METRO Group Asset Management geäußert haben. Sie wollten einerseits allgemein die Frage stellen, wie die Zukunft der Out-of-Town-Mall aussehen könnte und andererseits eine spezifische Antwort für Ümraniye suchen. Also haben wir uns zunächst gefragt, was denn die Probleme und möglichen Potenziale der Out-of-Town-Mall-Typologie in der Gegenwart und Zukunft sein könnten. Wir wollten also erst einen neuen Prototypen für diese Typologie entwickeln und diesen dann für Ümraniye interpretieren.

Auf dem Workshop in Istanbul: die beteiligten Architekten auf einem Blick
At the workshop in Istanbul: all of the architects involved

How did the invited firms work on the spot? Didn't the time become very short for everyone in the end?

All the competing firms from Germany, England and Turkey had arrived with two or three participants, but they each had a larger team at their headquarters who were working away for them at a distance. This was not the case with us. First there were two, then three of us there, but in London everyone was busy that weekend with other deadlines. As with every competition, things of course always get a bit tight in the end, so we did not manage to show our final design to our colleagues in London once more before we made our presentation. But this has happened to us quite a few times before in London. Our projects are often scattered over several continents, and so we learn to conduct our design discussions by email, telephone and fax as well.

How important is internal discussion? How important is it to FOA that all your designs have a typical, recognizable handwriting?

At FOA there is no rigid formal handwriting, and there is no interest in developing a fixed handwriting of this kind. Neither is there a genius with a pencil, whose subordinates have to make tracings of his sketches. But what we do have is a certain way of understanding, discussing and researching projects, and developing designs out of our realizations and letting them grow..

Can you explain this method using the example of Istanbul? How did you proceed there?

From the start we tackled in great detail the basic problems that METRO Group Asset Management articulated to us. On the one hand, they wanted to pose the general question of what the future of the out-of-town mall could look like, and on the other they were seeking a specific solution for Ümraniye. So first of all we asked ourselves what the problems and potentials of the out-of-town mall typology might be in the present and the future. We wanted first to develop a new prototype for this typology and then interpret this for Ümraniye.

And what problems and potentials of the traditional malls did you encounter?

A few disadvantages of the out-of-town mall have been known in Europe for a long time: big boxes with huge car parks, often architecturally unambitious, not easy to convert or to extend, contributing little to the local identity. But not only Europe has a great need for new complexes of this kind, but also Turkey, the Near East, India, Vietnam, Russia and China. That is why our work is not interested in the theoretical repair of the European mistakes of the 1970s and 1990s. We were interested in about the well-known failures, but also in further developing the old typology for the newly emerging metropolises in the Middle and Far East. In a time of explosive growth in urban development the question is often posed as to where exactly the city's limits are. What is called 'out of town' today cannot be called so any more in a couple of years' time, because the next wave of urban expansion has taken over the last suburb. This is why we found it important to ask what happens when an out-of-

*Und auf welche Probleme und Potenziale herkömmlicher Malls sind Sie dabei ge-
stoßen?*

Einige Nachteile der Out-of-Town-Mall sind in Europa seit Langem bekannt: große
Boxen mit riesigen Parkplätzen, oft ohne architektonische Ambitionen, schlecht um-
zunutzen oder zu erweitern, wenig beitragend zur lokalen Ortsidentität. Doch den
großen Bedarf an neuen Komplexen dieser Art hat nicht Europa, sondern haben die
Türkei, der Nahe Osten, Indien, Vietnam, Russland und China. Von daher ist unsere
Arbeit nicht interessiert an der theoretischen Reparatur der europäischen Fehler aus
den 1970er oder 1990er Jahren. Uns interessierte, von den bekannten Fehlern zu
lernen, aber auch die alte Typologie für die neu entstehenden Metropolen im Mittle-
ren und Fernen Osten weiterzuentwickeln. In einer Zeit des explosiven Wachstums
an Urbanität stellt sich oft die Frage, wo denn eigentlich die Grenze der Stadt ist. Was
heute „out-of-town" heißt, kann man in ein oder zwei Jahren oft nicht mehr so nennen, weil die nächste Welle der Stadterweiterung den letzten Vorort eingeholt hat.
Daher fanden wir es wichtig, zu fragen, was passiert, wenn eine Out-of-Town-Mall
auf einmal Teil einer Innenstadt wird und wie man diese Typologie weiterentwickeln
kann, um genau diese neuen Potenziale auszuschöpfen. Was wir erreichen wollen,
ist eine Evolution der Out-of-Town-Mall in ein urbanes Stadtzentrum für wachsende
Metropolen, eine Keimzelle für neue Plätze der Öffentlichkeit und für die lokale Identität in rapide wachsenden Ballungszentren.

Können Sie die Bestandteile Ihres Prototypen beschreiben?

Der Prototyp definiert die Art und Weise, wie Anchorstores platziert werden und
Shops sowie öffentliche Plätze sich miteinander verbinden und wachsen können.
Auf folgende Kriterien könnte man den Prototyp reduzieren: Um als urbaner Platz zu
funktionieren, muss es mindestens drei unterschiedliche Routen geben, die auf und
durch das Gelände führen; es müssen über 1000 Parkplätze vorhanden sein, aber
die Parkfläche für Autos muss sich unter oder über dem Niveau der öffentlichen Ebene, jedoch nie ebenerdig befinden; des Weiteren sollten die Dachflächen als fünfte
Fassade entworfen werden, sie müssen nicht zwingend begrünt sein, aber das Dach
muss wenigstens in Teilen begehbar sein und von Menschen, nicht von Haustechnik
genutzt werden.

Ist Ihr Prototyp auf sämtliche Out-of-Town-Malls anwendbar?

Nein, der neue Prototyp ist in seiner jetzigen Form nicht für Europa geeignet. Er ist
anwendbar auf Städte, die in einem rasanten Tempo wachsen. In Europa spricht man
hingegen eher von schrumpfenden Städten oder von der Regenerierung der alten
Stadtzentren. Ein derart exzessives Wachstum wie etwa in Ümraniye gibt es hingegen nicht. Von daher ist es ein spezifischer Prototyp.

town mall suddenly becomes part of the inner city, and how one can further develop this typology to make use of exactly this potential. What we want to achieve is an evolution of the out-of-town mall into an urban city centre for growing metropolises, a nucleus for new public areas and for the local identity in rapidly growing centres of population.

Can you describe the components of your prototype?

The prototype defines the way in which anchor stores are placed and shops and public squares can be combined and grow together. The prototype could be reduced to the following criteria: In order to function as an urban square, there must be at least three different routes which lead to and through the area; there must be more than 1,000 parking spaces, but the car park must be below or above the level of the public area, but never at ground level; in addition, the roof surfaces should be designed as a fifth façade; they do not need to be grassed over, but the roof should be accessible at least in part, and used by people, not by domestic engineering.

Is your prototype applicable to all out-of-town malls?

No, the new prototype in its present form is not suitable for Europe. It is applicable to cities that are growing at lightning speed. In Europe on the contrary people are speaking of shrinking cities, or of the regeneration of the old city centres. But there is no excessive growth such as, for example, in Ümraniye. This is why it is a specific prototype.

What were the challenges that confronted you in applying the prototype to Ümraniye?

The topography of the site for example, that is, the elevation differences of the premises. We wanted to allow access to the complex on several levels, without major formal dislocation. Another difficulty was that we did not know what would be happening over the next few years on the neighbouring sites. It was important to us to plan access routes and streets that could link us and our neighbours into an urban structure. But of course we could not force any of the neighbours to work with us and plan streets that would link us together. But what we can do is provide potential, possible access to the context – with the hope that at least some of the neighbours will show interest in the future.

Can you explain this further?

The German word *Sollbruchstelle* (predetermined breaking point) has proved very helpful in explaining what we want to achieve. The blocks we have planned have three *Sollbruchstellen*. And if the neighbours show interest in the future, then it will be possible at little expense to 'break up' the blocks at these points and create new streets which extend into the context. In this way we were trying to design a complex which looks like a completed project at the access point, but contains potential in its basic structure that extends far beyond this complex.

Blick auf das Grundstück in Ümraniye, für das FOA einen Prototypen entwickelte
View of the site in Ümraniye for which FOA developed a prototype

Mit welchen Herausforderungen waren Sie konfrontiert, als Sie den Prototypen auf Ümraniye anwenden wollten?

Mit der Topografie der Site zum Beispiel, also dem Höhenunterschied des Geländes. Wir wollten, dass man auf mehreren Niveaus in das Projekt hineinkommen kann – ohne größere formale Verrenkungen. Schwierig war auch, dass man nicht weiß, was auf den benachbarten Grundstücken in den nächsten Jahren passieren wird. Es war uns wichtig, Öffnungen und Straßen zu planen, die uns und die Nachbarn in eine Stadtstruktur einbinden könnten. Aber natürlich können wir keinen der Nachbarn zwingen, mit uns zusammen zu arbeiten und Straßen zu planen, die uns verbinden. Was wir jedoch tun können ist das Bereitstellen von Potenzialen, von möglichen Öffnungen zum Kontext – mit der Hoffnung, dass zumindest einige der Nachbarn in Zukunft Interesse zeigen werden.

Können Sie das näher erklären?

Das deutsche Wort „Sollbruchstelle" hat sich als sehr hilfreich erwiesen, um zu erklären, was wir erreichen wollten. Die von uns geplanten Blöcke haben drei „Sollbruchstellen". Und wenn die Nachbarn in der Zukunft Interesse zeigen, dann wird es möglich sein, mit geringem Aufwand die Blöcke an diesen Stellen „aufzubrechen" und neue Straßen zu formen, die in den Kontext hineinreichen. Auf diese Weise versuchten wir, ein Projekt zu entwerfen, das bei seiner Eröffnung wie ein fertiges Projekt erscheint, aber in seiner Grundstruktur Potenziale beinhaltet, die weit über dieses Projekt hinausreichen.

Was war – im Vergleich zu den anderen Entwürfen für Ümraniye – das Spezifische an Ihrem Modell?

Die meisten Entwürfe haben sich mehr mit der architektonischen Erscheinung und weniger mit dem urbanen Potenzial beschäftigt. Wir waren vielleicht weniger daran interessiert, dass eine Architektur herauskommt, die man formal einfach beschreiben kann, und mehr daran, Architektur über die Verbindungen und Formen des öffentlichen Raums zu definieren. Ein Ansatz, der typisch ist für die Arbeiten von FOA, wie man etwa beim Yokohama Projekt oder dem South-East-Coastal Park in Barcelona gut erkennen kann – alles eher urbane Landschaften, aus Oberflächen gewachsene Formen, die nicht darauf ausgelegt sind, ein Bild oder Icon zu produzieren.

Viele bekannte Gebäude erhalten ihre urbane Signifikanz aus ihrer Silhouette. Doch urbaner Raum ist ein weiterer Weg, Räume zu entwerfen, die eine wichtige Rolle in der Identität der Stadt einnehmen. In vielen unserer Projekte ist das Verhältnis zum öffentlichen Raum eine wichtige konzeptionelle Geste des Entwurfes. Für das Yokohama Terminal zum Beispiel hatten wir im Wettbewerb vorgeschlagen, die normale „Einbahnstraße" der Bewegungen im Terminal zu ändern, indem wir einen öffentlichen Platz und Park auf das Dach und den öffentlichsten Teil des Programms, das Konferenzzentrum, an das letzte Ende des Platzes legten. Mit diesen zwei Vorschlägen schafften wir es, ein stilles, oft leeres Terminal in einen Ort für die ganze Stadt

Urbane Landschaft: der South East Coastal Park in Barcelona
Urban landscape: South East Coastal Park, Barcelona

Most of the designs were concerned more with architectural appearance and less with urban potential. We were perhaps less concerned with producing an architecture which can be simply be described in formal terms, and more with defining architecture in terms of the links and forms of public space.

An approach that is typical of the work of FOA, as can be recognized for example in the Yokohama Project or the South-East Coastal Park in Barcelona – all basically urban landscapes, forms that have grown up out of the surfaces, which are not designed to produce an image of an icon. Many well-known buildings gain their urban significance from their silhouette. But urban space is a further way of designing spaces that take up an important role in the identity of the city. In many of our projects the relationship with public space is an important conceptual element of the design. For the Yokohama Terminal, for example, we suggested in the competition changing the normal 'one-way street' of movement in the terminal by putting a public square and park on the roof and the most public part of the programme, the conference centre, at the far end of the square. With these two suggestions we managed to transform a quiet, often empty terminal into a place for the whole city, with conference participants, tourists and people just going for a walk in almost all corners of the building and roof. As one can see with the Yokohama Project too, an important part of these new public spaces in many cases is the breaking up of clear boundaries between different programmes that are otherwise separated.

Can you perhaps explain how this applies to Meydan?

Here, what was important to us, for example, was to get rid of the car park, because this otherwise creates a distance between the buildings that cannot be filled with any life. But a gigantic, dark underground car park is not necessarily a better solution. Turkish motorists don't like to park underground; they would rather take a detour if it enables them to park at ground level near the entrance. Hence we had to design the parking area so that customers accepted the parking spaces under Meydan as at least equivalent to the ground-level parking area of Ikea next door. This is why the surfaces are formed, folded and cut so that the central square lies in the middle, halfway between the car park and the upper surface. Thus we wanted to break up the separation between the underground car park, the shops and the public space in such a way that the car park no longer feels like a separate underground area to the customer, but like an extension of the public space.

What else is important to bring an artificially created public square actually to life?

Almost all public squares began as crossroads, as we can see for example in the Alexanderplatz or the Potsdamer Platz in Berlin. It was the square at the gateway to which all streets led. This was where there was the greatest density of people, who came from all directions and lingered – and in that way the crossroads gradually became a square. New squares function better when they retain the potential of a crossroads, when they lie on the natural route of a number of people – and thus are more than an arbitrary gap in the urban network.

zu verwandeln, mit Spaziergängern, Konferenzteilnehmern und Touristen in fast allen Winkeln des Gebäudes und Daches. Wie man auch beim Yokohama Projekt sehen kann, ist ein wichtiger Teil dieser neuen öffentlichen Räume in vielen Fällen das Aufbrechen von klaren Grenzen zwischen verschiedenen Programmen, die sonst getrennt werden.

Können Sie das vielleicht am Beispiel Meydan erläutern?

Uns war hier zum Beispiel wichtig, dass der Parkplatz verschwindet, weil dieser sonst eine Distanz schafft zwischen den Gebäuden, die mit keinem Leben zu füllen ist. Aber eine riesige dunkle Tiefgarage ist nicht unbedingt eine so viel bessere Lösung. Türkische Autofahrer parken nicht gern unter der Erde, sie fahren lieber Umwege, wenn sie dafür ebenerdig neben der Eingangstür parken können. Wir mussten das Parken demnach so gestalten, dass die Kunden die Parkplätze unter dem Meydan als mindestens gleichwertig akzeptieren zu der ebenerdigen Parkfläche vor Ikea nebenan. Darum sind die Oberflächen so geformt, gefaltet und geschnitten, dass der zentrale Platz in der Mitte auf halbem Weg zwischen dem Parkplatz und der Oberfläche liegt. Wir wollten also die Trennung zwischen Tiefgarage, Läden und öffentlichem Raum so aufbrechen, dass sich die Tiefgarage für den Kunden nicht mehr wie ein separater Untergrund anfühlt, sondern wie eine Erweiterung des öffentlichen Raums.

Was ist sonst noch wichtig, damit ein künstlich geschaffener öffentlicher Platz tatsächlich lebendig wird?

Fast alle öffentlichen Plätze haben einmal als Kreuzung angefangen, wie man etwa am Alexanderplatz oder am Potsdamer Platz in Berlin gut erkennen kann. Es war der Platz vor dem Tor, auf den alle Straßen zuführten. Hier hatte man die größte Dichte von Menschen, die aus allen Richtungen kamen und verweilten – so wurde die Kreuzung langsam zum Platz. Neue Plätze funktionieren dann besser, wenn sie das Potenzial einer Kreuzung beinhalten, wenn sie auf der natürlichen Route einer Vielzahl von Menschen liegen – und somit mehr sind als eine willkürliche Aussparung im Stadtgewebe.

Was bedeutet diese Erkenntnis für Shopping Malls, die ja in der Regel gerade mal über eine Ein- und Ausfahrt verfügen?

In dem Zusammenhang sind Shoppingcenter, also die klassischen Out-of-Town-Malls, natürlich schwierig: Mit den beiden Wegen für Autos entsteht keine Kreuzung und erst recht kein Platz. Daher war es für uns wichtig, weitere Arten des Bewegens neben dem Auto zuzulassen und zu stärken. Aus der Nachbarschaft wollen vielleicht einige zu Fuß kommen oder mit dem Fahrrad. Und wenn man Wege für diese Leute schafft, wie wir das mit der Verbindung über das Dach gemacht haben, könnte das Gebäude mehr werden als ein herkömmliches Shoppingcenter mit

In this context shopping centres, that is the classic out-of-town malls, are of course difficult. With the two routes for cars, there is no crossroads and certainly no square. So it was important for us to allow and strengthen other forms of movement apart from by car. Some people from the neighbourhood might perhaps want to come on foot or by bicycle. And if routes are created for these people, as we did with the link via the roof, the building could become more than a traditional shopping centre with a food court, where one could quickly eat an ice cream and then get back into the car. A public square could evolve which could become part of the city, or the core of a new centre. At the moment there are already four different routes to get to the site. If in the future the surrounding development is completed and the access points to the neighbouring sites that we have envisaged are realized, it could be six or seven. And through these many routes it also very quickly becomes clear that the shopping centre is not a closed complex, related only to itself. While other malls often define their roles as a private site with signs and security fences, these elements will not exist in Meydan.

A square where only a few people are moving can soon appear empty and dreary. How do you ensure that people feel at ease in a square, even when there is not such a great crowd?

The square should contain enough elements so that smaller spaces can emerge, so that it functions just as well on a normal Tuesday morning as for a Turkish wedding with many hundreds of guests. Five elements are important here in Meydan: steps that are as high as a bench for seating and which therefore encourage people to linger; trees whose crowns form a more local canopy; more benches on the lower areas, lighting to create varying atmospheres after twilight; and water features for coolness and for acoustic reasons.

Is it important for the square to have a visual identity?

We have tried to create a combination of one and multiple identities. The central area of the square is defined by various identities that grow into the square. This was the reason for the pockets, the depressions in the square at each of the corners. There we created zones that are part of the large square, but they are so small and narrow that they can be seen as mini-squares. Casual World for example could build a catwalk for an event that begins in their little square and extends into the centre of the large square. Or Sportsworld could set up a skateboard ramp which begins in their part and leads down into the square.

Isn't it very brave of you to plan a shopping centre in the open air?

Traditionally malls are roofed over, so that customers can stroll and shop at all times, protected from wind and weather.

einem Foodcourt, wo man noch schnell ein Eis isst und dann zurück ins Auto steigt. Ein öffentlicher Platz könnte so entstehen, der ein Teil der Stadt oder der Kern eines neuen Zentrums werden kann. Momentan gibt es bereits vier verschiedene Routen, um auf das Grundstück zu gelangen. Wenn in Zukunft die umliegende Bebauung fertig ist und die Durchbrüche zu den Nachbargrundstücken, die wir konzipiert haben, realisiert werden, könnten es sechs oder sieben werden. Und durch diese vielen Wege wird auch sehr schnell klar, dass es sich bei dem Shoppingcenter nicht um einen abgeschlossenen, nur auf sich selbst bezogenen Komplex handelt. Während andere Malls oft ihre Rolle als Privatgrundstück mit Schildern und Sicherheitszaun definieren, wird es solche Elemente bei Meydan nicht geben.

Ein Platz, auf den sich nur wenige Menschen bewegen, wirkt schnell leer und trist. Wie schafft man es, dass sich die Leute dort auch dann wohl fühlen, wenn der Andrang nicht so groß ist?

Der Platz sollte genug Elemente enthalten, um kleinere Räume entstehen zu lassen, damit er an einem normalen Dienstagvormittag genauso gut funktioniert wie für eine türkische Hochzeit mit vielen hundert Gästen. Fünf Elemente sind dafür wichtig in Meydan: Stufen, welche die Höhe einer Sitzbank haben und somit zum Verweilen einladen; Bäume, deren Kronen ein lokaleres Dach bilden; des Weiteren Bänke auf den flacheren Bereichen, Lichter zur Schaffung von unterschiedlichen Atmosphären nach der Dämmerung und Wasserspiele zur Kühlung und aus akustischen Gründen.

Ist es wichtig, dass der Platz eine visuelle Identität hat?

Wir haben versucht, eine Mischung zwischen einer und multiplen Identitäten zu schaffen. Der zentrale Bereich des Platzes wird definiert von verschiedenen Identitäten, die in den Platz hineinwachsen. Das war der Grund für die Pockets, die Vertiefungen in der Platzform an den jeweiligen Ecken. Dort entstanden Zonen, die zwar Teil des großen Platzes sind, aber wiederum so eng und klein sind, dass man sie auch als Miniplätze verstehen kann. Die Casual World zum Beispiel könnte für einen Event einen Laufsteg bauen, der in ihrem kleinen Platz beginnt und in die Mitte des großen Platzes hinausragt. Oder Sportsworld könnte eine Skateboardrampe aufstellen, die in ihrem Teil beginnt und hinab auf den Platz führt.

Ist es nicht sehr mutig, ein Shoppingcenter unter freiem Himmel zu planen?

Traditionell gehört ein Dach über die Mall, weil damit der Kunde vor Wind und Wetter geschützt zu jeder Zeit flanieren und einkaufen kann.
Der Trend – vor allem in Amerika – ging in den letzten Jahren zurück zur Interpretation der klassischen High-Street-Typologie. Allerdings nicht zur alten, gewachsenen High Street, sondern man baut Malls, die wie High Streets aussehen und funktionieren. Diese Malls sind alle open air und geben den Mietern wieder die Möglichkeit, sich stärker als durch einzelne Läden in Szene zu setzen. Was wir vorgeschlagen

The trend – above all in America – in recent years has been to go back to the interpretation of the classic high street typology. Admittedly not to the old, naturally developed high street, but malls are being built that look and function like high streets. These malls are all open-air and once again give tenants the opportunity to put themselves in the limelight more strongly than by means of individual shops. What we have proposed is a combination of the classic models. On the one hand, there is a small roofed mall opposite the Real supermarket, and on the other hand the shops on the square. The path to the shops is roofed over, and the roofs overhang by four to eight metres. So even in heavy rain, one would be in the dry when moving from the car to each shop and back again to the car. Apart from rain, we spent a long time tackling the problem of wind. There is often a very strong wind blowing through Ümraniye. For this reason we put our model through several computer wind-tunnel tests. The reason why the cinema folds upwards geometrically to the square for example has to do with the fact that we needed a change in profile to ensure that wind speeds remain comfortable at ground level.

The development of the shopping centre began with the idea of the Austrian architect Viktor Gruen, who wanted to create a centre for people in the rapidly developing suburbs of America, a social place where neighbours could meet and stroll. Unfortunately this aspect was neglected in the subsequent development of the mall, while the commercial one moved into the foreground. When one now looks at Meydan, one is reminded of Gruen and his visions. In which way did Gruen's ideas influence your work?

As we discovered, admittedly only after the Istanbul workshop, after the First World War Viktor Gruen actually made similar drawings to ours on the themes of parking and shopping. In one of his first prototypes he had the car park on the roof and the entrance to the shopping area right in the middle. Although Gruen developed very American models, his aspirations were similar to ours. He experimented with many things that we are also experimenting with. I am impressed above all with how he attempted to work with the boundary between public space and window displays; his work in this field was far ahead of his time. Gruen did not see himself as an architect who won commissions because of his handwriting and the way in which he designed façades, rather he was interested in the way that space and the interplay of programmes function. In this respect he is closer to FOA than most other architects of his time.

When one looks at Meydan in the context of other FOA projects, in which respects were you able to draw on your experiences with other designs? With which projects of FOA does Meydan most closely resonate?

We don't try to transfer details and ideas from one project to the next. Each project is developed according to its specific demands. But of course there are also projects that have had similar contexts and therefore perhaps demanded similar solutions. West Quay III in Southampton is not dissimilar in some ways, because the city there, just as with Meydan, had no public square and was in search of its identity and its centre. Another project where, however, no public square was required, but we decided to establish one there, is the Yokohama Project. The difficult thing here was that we were dealing with a context that could not be precisely defined. Sometimes

haben, ist eine Mischung der klassischen Modelle. Es gibt einerseits eine kleine überdachte Mall gegenüber von Real und andererseits die Shops am Platz. Der Weg zu den Shops ist überdacht, die Dächer kragen zwischen vier und acht Meter aus. Selbst bei starkem Regen käme man also im Trockenen vom Auto zu jedem Laden und wieder zurück zum Wagen. Neben dem Regen haben wir uns länger mit dem Wind auseinandergesetzt. In Ümraniye bläst oft ein sehr starker Nordwind. Daher ist unser Modell durch mehrere Computer-Windtunneltests gegangen. Der Grund, warum das Kino sich in der Geometrie auffaltet zum Platz, hat zum Beispiel damit zu tun, dass wir eine Änderung im Profil brauchten, um sicher zu stellen, dass die Windgeschwindigkeiten am Boden komfortabel bleiben.

Begonnen hat die Entwicklung der Shoppingcenter mit der Idee des österreichischen Architekten Viktor Gruen, der in den sich schnell entwickelnden Suburbs von Amerika für die Menschen ein Zentrum schaffen wollte, einen sozialen Platz, wo sich die Nachbarn treffen und flanieren können. Leider wurde dieser Aspekt in der folgenden Entwicklung der Malls vernachlässigt, während der kommerzielle in den Vordergrund rückte. Wenn man sich nun Meydan anschaut, fühlt man sich an Gruen und seine Visionen erinnert. Welchen Einfluß hatten Gruens Ansätze auf Ihre Arbeit?

Wie wir allerdings erst nach dem Workshop in Istanbul entdeckten, hat Victor Gruen nach dem Zweiten Weltkrieg zum Thema Parken und Einkaufen sogar schon ähnliche Zeichnungen gemacht wie wir. Bei einem seiner ersten Prototypen hatte er das Parking auf das Dach und den Eingang zum Kaufhaus direkt in die Mitte gesetzt. Obwohl Gruen sehr amerikanische Modelle entwickelte, war die Aspiration ähnlich der unseren. Er hat mit vielen Dingen experimentiert, mit denen wir auch experimentie-

ren. Mich beeindruckt vor allem, wie er versucht hat, mit der Grenze zwischen öffentlichem Raum und Schaufenstern zu arbeiten, seine Arbeit auf diesem Feld war seiner Zeit weit voraus. Gruen sah sich nicht als Architekt, der durch seine Handschrift und die Art und Weise, wie er Fassaden macht, Projekte gewann, vielmehr interessierte ihn, wie der Raum und das Zusammenspiel von Programmen funktionieren. In dieser Hinsicht ist er FOA näher als die meisten anderen Architekten seiner Zeit.

Wenn man Meydan im Kontext der anderen Projekte von FOA betrachtet: In welchen Aspekten konnte man auf Erfahrungen bei anderen Entwürfen zurückgreifen? Mit welchen Arbeiten von FOA räsoniert Meydan am ehesten?

Wir versuchen nicht, Details und Ideen von einem Projekt zum nächsten zu tragen. Jedes Projekt wird aus seinen spezifischen Herausforderungen entwickelt. Aber natürlich gibt es auch Projekte, die ähnliche Kontexte hatten und von daher vielleicht ähnliche Antworten erforderten. Das West Quay III in Southampton ist etwa in mancherlei Hinsicht nicht unähnlich, weil die Stadt dort ebenso wie Meydan keinen öffentlichen Platz hatte und sich auf der Suche nach ihrer Identität und ihrem Zentrum befand. Ein anderes Projekt, wo zwar kein öffentlicher Platz gefragt war, wir uns aber

there is a cruise ship moored only on one side, sometimes on both sides or even on neither. What we tried to do at Yokohama as well as later at Meydan was to abolish the strict separation of functions between different programmes. So the way in which the port terminal and the park are linked together are clearly characterized by the need to create seamless transitions, in order to set as few boundaries as possible to the differing and often incalculable uses of the area. As far as the façade is concerned, we had a similar problem with Meydan to the one we had with the High-cross Quarter in Leicester and to some extent with the Museum of Contemporary Art in Cleveland. The question was: how can one wrap, ornament or disguise a building if the internal programme demands nothing of the façade in functional terms? Malls and cinemas in general have no questions, no demands on the façade. This is a problem that we have encountered with several projects and that each time requires specific solutions. With both cinemas, the one in Leicester and the one in Ümraniye, we are playing with the space between the cinema box and the escape corridor and asking how we can use or alter this space – by means of light for example, or the sculptural deformation of this space.

What do you think can be achieved by Meydan?

I would be pleased if the project could be seen as an alternative to the way that shopping centres have been built up to now, if Meydan could provide a stimulus for new, different ways of building a mall. I hope that this project for Istanbul and Ümraniye can be more than a shopping centre, that it influences the development of the neighbouring sites and that in doing so it succeeds in giving Ümraniye a centre and an urban identity.

Unbestimmter Kontext: Fährterminal von FOA in Yokohama (links und unten)
Undetermined context: ferry terminal by FOA in Yokohama (left and below)

entschieden haben, einen dort zu etablieren, ist das Yokohama Projekt. Das Schwierige hierbei war, dass wir es mit einem Kontext zu tun hatten, den man nicht genau bestimmen kann. Manchmal liegt nur an einer Seite ein Kreuzfahrtschiff, manchmal auf beiden oder auch mal keins. Was wir bei Yokohama wie auch später dann bei Meydan versucht haben, ist die Aufhebung der strikten Funktionstrennung zwischen verschiedenen Programmen. Also die Art und Weise, wie sich das Fährterminal und der Park sowie Terminal und die Parkfläche miteinander verbinden, ist klar geprägt vom Bedürfnis, nahtlose Übergänge zu schaffen, um den unterschiedlichen und oft unberechenbaren Nutzungen so wenig Grenzen wie möglich zu setzen. Was die Fassade betrifft, so hatten wir bei Meydan ein ähnliches Problem wie beim Highcross Quarter in Leicester und zum Teil beim Museum of Contemporary Art in Cleveland. Die Frage war: Wie kann man ein Gebäude umhüllen, ornamentieren oder verkleiden, wenn das interne Programm nichts Funktionales von der Fassade möchte? Malls und Kinos haben in der Regel keine Fragen, keine Bedürfnisse an die Fassade. Das ist ein Problem, das wir bei mehreren Projekten angetroffen haben und das jedes Mal wieder seine spezifischen Lösungen sucht. Bei beiden Kinos, dem in Leicester und dem in Ümraniye, spielen wir mit dem Raum zwischen der Kinobox und dem Fluchtkorridor und fragen, wie man diesen Raum nutzen oder performen kann – durch Licht zum Beispiel, oder das skulpturale Verformen dieses Raumes.

Was, glauben Sie, kann Meydan bewirken?

Es würde mich freuen, wenn das Projekt gesehen wird als Alternative dazu, wie man Shoppingcenter bisher gebaut hat, wenn Meydan Anregungen gibt für neue, andere Arten, eine Mall zu bauen. Ich hoffe, dass dieses Projekt für Istanbul und Ümraniye mehr sein kann als ein Shoppingcenter, dass es die Entwicklung der benachbarten Grundstücke beeinflusst und dass es gelingt, Ümraniye hiermit ein Zentrum und eine urbane Identität zu geben.

DIE HERAUSFORDERUNG
THE CHALLENGE

WÄRME Mit dem Urknall fing es an: Von der Akkretion, der Entstehung der Erde vor ca. 4,6 bis 4,7 Milliarden Jahren, ist immer noch so viel Restwärme übrig, dass man heute damit ganze Siedlungen und Städte beheizen und mit Strom versorgen kann. Geothermie – oder Erdwärme – nennt man die im oberen Teil der Erdkruste gespeicherte Wärme, die zunehmend als Energiequelle genutzt wird. Nahezu unerschöpflich ist der Ofen unter unseren Füßen. Experten gehen davon aus, dass die Wärme von Mutter Erde den heutigen Weltenergiebedarf für 30 Millionen Jahre decken könnte.

Doch die Nutzung von Erdenergie ist so neu nicht. Schon die Gallier, Kelten und Germanen wärmten im heißen Thermalquellwasser ihre Speisen. Vor 2000 Jahren leiteten die alten Römer das warme Wasser nicht nur in marmorne Becken, um darin zu baden, sondern auch in unterirdischen Kanälen unter den Häusern entlang – das Prinzip der Fußbodenheizung war erfunden. In dem französischen Dorf Chaudes-Aigues wurde im 14. Jahrhundert das erste städtische Wärmenetz installiert: In hölzernen Rohren floss das über 80 Grad Celsius heiße Thermalwasser in die Häuser. Heute kann man sich das historische System in einem Museum vor Ort noch erklären lassen. Das allererste Erdwärmekraftwerk entstand hingegen vor fast 100 Jahren in der Toskana. Da wo die afrikanische und die eurasische Kontinentalplatte aufeinandertreffen, heizt Magma oberflächennahe, unterirdische Wasserreservoire auf. Graf Piero Ginori Conti nutzte dieses Phänomen zur Stromerzeugung, indem er den hier und da aus dem Boden aufsteigenden Wasserdampf Turbinen antreiben ließ. 1913 brachte das erste Erdwärmekraftwerk der Welt 220 Kilowatt Leistung. Heute werden hier 400 Megawatt Strom in Italiens Energienetz eingespeist.

Dass Geothermie erst in den letzten Jahrzehnten als Energiequelle wiederentdeckt wurde, kann vor dem Hintergrund der Klimadebatte erklärt werden. Als Alternative zu anderen Formen der Energiegewinnung, vor allem denen mit fossilen Brennstoffen, hat die Nutzung von Erdwärme einige entscheidende Vorteile: Sie steht unabhängig von der Tages- und Jahreszeit oder den herrschenden Klimabedingungen zur Verfügung; da sie direkt vor Ort zu finden ist, benötigt man keine aufwendigen Transportsysteme; und umweltverschmutzende Nebenprodukte entstehen auch nicht. Nach den Vorstellungen der Branche werden durch Geothermie bis zum Jahr 2020 sogar mehr als 20 Millionen Tonnen Kohlendioxid eingespart. Mit Erdwärme gegen die Erderwärmung – könnte man da als Slogan formulieren.

Unterschieden wird zwischen der Tiefengeothermie und der oberflächennahen Geothermie. Bei der ersten Variante gräbt sich der Bohrer zuweilen drei bis vier Kilometer tief in den Boden, um auf so heißes Wasser zu stoßen, dass man es zur Stromgewinnung nutzen kann. Dafür sollte es mindestens 100 Grad Celsius heiß sein. Weltweit sind schon etwa 250 Geothermiekraftwerke in Betrieb. Bei der oberflächennahen Geothermie hingegen gehen die Bohrungen selten tiefer als 150 Meter in die Erde. Hier ist die Temperatur nicht so hoch, oft nur acht bis zwölf Grad. Neben der Wärmepumpe, welche die benötigten höheren Tem-

HEAT   It began with the Big Bang. From the accretion, the formation of the earth about 4.6 to 4.7 billion years ago, enough residual heat still remains to heat whole settlements and cities and supply them with electricity. Geothermy or terrestrial heat is the name given to the heat stored in the upper part of the earth's crust, which is increasingly used as a source of energy. This furnace beneath our feet is practically inexhaustible. Experts estimate that the heat of Mother Earth could cover the entire world demand for 30 million years.

But the use of geothermal power is not that new. The Gauls, Celts and Teutons heated their food in the water of hot thermal springs. The ancient Romans, 2000 years ago, directed their hot water not only into marble basins in order to bathe in it, but also into underwater channels under the houses – and thus underfloor heating was invented. In the fourteenth century, the first urban heating system was installed in the French village of Chaudes-Aigues. The thermal water, at a heat of 80 degrees Celsius, flowed into the houses through wooden pipes. Today this historic system can be studied in a local museum. The very first geothermal power plant on the other hand was built almost 100 years ago in Tuscany. Where the African and Eurasian continental plates meet, underground water reservoirs near the earth's surface are heated by magma. Count Piero Ginori Conti used this phenomenon to create electric current by means of turbines powered by the steam that rose here and there from the earth. In 1913, the first geothermal power plant in the world produced 220 kilowatts. Today 400 megawatts of power are fed into Italy's energy grid.

That it was only in recent decades that terrestrial heat has been redeveloped as a source of energy can be explained by the background of the climate debate. As an alternative to other forms of energy generation, above all those with fossil fuels, the use of terrestrial heat has some decisive advantages: It is available independently of the time of day or year, or the current climatic conditions; since it is to be found directly on the spot, there is no need of costly transport systems; and it does not produce environmental pollution. According to the industry, geothermal heating will even have saved more than 20 million tonnes of carbon dioxide by the year 2020. Earth heat against global warming – it could become a slogan.

A distinction is made between deep geothermy and shallow geothermy (close to the surface). With the first type, the drill sometimes penetrates three or four kilometres deep into the earth, in order to find water hot enough to be used as a source of power. For this purpose it needs to be at least 100 degrees Celsius. Worldwide there are already about 250 geothermal power stations operating. With geothermy near the surface, however, the drilling seldom goes deeper than 150 metres into the earth. Here the temperature is not as hot, often only eight to twelve degrees. Apart from the heat pump which creates the required necessary high temperatures, a geothermal probe is necessary, filled with a heat-transfer fluid, which heats the building by means of the heat pump. But geothermal power not only heats the home: It can also be

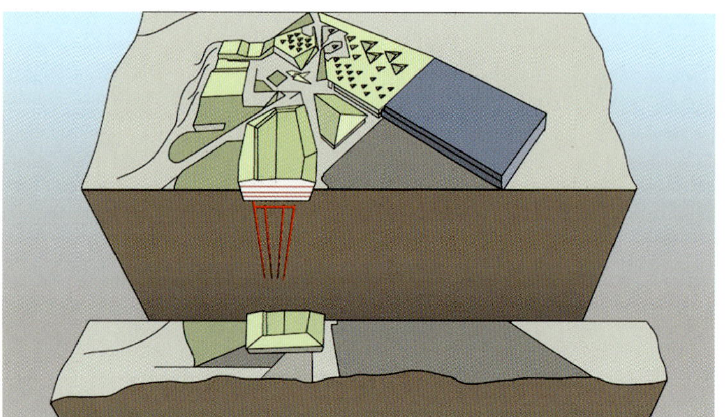

Bohrungen zum Mittelpunkt der Erde: Skizze für die Geothermieanlage von
Meydan (oben links) und praktische Umsetzung auf der Baustelle (rechts)
Drilling to the centre of the earth: sketch by Meydan of the geothermal
complex (above left) and in practice on the building site (right)

peraturen erzeugt, ist eine Erdwärmesonde notwendig, die mit einer Wärmeträgerflüssigkeit gefüllt ist und
in Verbindung mit einer Wärmepumpe das Gebäude heizt. Aber nicht nur warm wird das Haus durch die
Energie aus der Erde: Auch Klimakälte kann aus dem Boden kommen. Dabei wird nur die in der Anlage zir-
kulierende Wärmeträgerflüssigkeit genutzt bzw. mit Pumpen im Gebäude umgewälzt. Der Energieaufwand
beschränkt sich auf den Stromverbrauch ebendieser Pumpen, herkömmliche Aggregate zur Erzeugung von
Klimakälte entfallen. Mit einer Kilowattstunde elektrischer Energie können somit bis zu 100 Kilowattstunden thermischer Energie bereitgestellt werden.
Vor allem bei kleineren Gebäuden wie Einfamilienhäusern wird Geothermie angewendet. Mit Meydan in
Ümraniye, wo ein Großteil der für den Betrieb benötigten Wärme und Kühle aus der Erde kommt, wird
das Verfahren nun hingegen bei einem ungewöhnlich großen Objekt angewendet. Für die Türkei ist dieses
Projekt so einzigartig wie richtungsweisend – könnte das Land doch in den nächsten Jahren sehr stark
von Erdwärme profitieren. Die geografische Lage des Landes an der Grenze zweier Kontinentalplatten
birgt zwar einerseits eine ständige Erdbebengefahr, hat andererseits aber auch einen entscheidenden Vorteil: Erdwärmepotenziale sind hier größer als anderswo. Im Bereich der Plattengrenzen gelangt nämlich
wesentlich mehr Wärme aus dem Erdinneren in die Nähe der Oberfläche als in anderen Gebieten. Wis-
senschaftler sprechen in dem Zusammenhang von „geothermischen Anomalien". Hier können Temperatur-
unterschiede von 15 Grad Celsius pro 100 Meter Tiefenzunahme entstehen – normal sind eher drei Grad
pro 100 Meter.
Mit den Bohrungen für die Geothermieanlage begann die Bauphase von Meydan – und damit die erste
Herausforderung für Ingenieure wie Arbeiter. Nicht überall konnten sie so tief bohren wie geplant. Nicht
selten stießen sie auf halbem Weg auf Gestein. Also musste die Anzahl der Löcher erweitert werden, die
Arbeiten verzögerten sich. Für ein wenig Aufregung sorgte auch die Tatsache, dass eine NATO-Pipeline direkt unter Ümraniye entlangführt. Jedoch geht diese, wie bald mit großer Erleichterung festgestellt werden
konnte, knapp an dem Baugrundstück vorbei.

used for cooling. Here only the heat-transfer fluid circulating in the system is used, or it is recycled in the building by means of pumps. The use of energy is restricted to the current used by these pumps, while the traditional units used to create a cool atmosphere are not used. Thus one kilowatt-hour of electrical energy can create as much as 100 kilowatt-hours of thermal energy.

Geothermy is used above all for smaller buildings such as single-family dwellings. With 'Meydan' in Ümraniye, where the bigger part of the heat and cold necessary for running the system comes from the earth, this process is now applied to an unusually large structure. For Turkey, this project is as unique as it is trend-setting – after all, the country could make great profits over the next few years from terrestrial heat. The country's geographical position on the border of two continental plates on the one hand admittedly involves a continual threat of earthquakes, but on the other hand it also has one decisive advantage: Geothermal potential is greater here than anywhere else, for in the area of the plate boundaries more heat from the interior of the earth reaches the vicinity of the surface than in other areas. Scientists speak in this connection of 'geothermal anomalies'. Here temperature differences of 15 degrees Celsius per 100 metres of increase in depth can occur, as against a normal difference of three degrees per 100 metres.

The building phase of 'Meydan' began with the drilling for the geothermy system – and this represented the first challenge for both engineers and workers. They could not drill as deeply everywhere as had been planned. Often rock was struck halfway down. The number of drill holes therefore had to be increased, and the work was slowed down. To add a little excitement, it was also found that a NATO pipeline ran directly under Ümraniye. However, as was discovered to great general relief, this passes just to the side of the building site.

HERAUSFORDERUNGEN DER ARCHITEKTUR   Der Entwurf ist das eine, dessen Umsetzung das andere. Nicht alles, was Architekten in dreidimensionalen Programmen entwerfen, lässt sich ohne Probleme realisieren. Vor allem dann nicht, wenn es sich um eine so außergewöhnliche und unkonventionelle Architektur handelt wie die von FOA. Eine der größten Herausforderungen des Entwurfs war die Dachkonstruktion.

Die Statik liebt die Gleichmäßigkeit der Konstruktion: Dann nämlich ist das statische System relativ einfach zu berechnen. Doch der Entwurf von Meydan ist alles andere als gleichmäßig, gehört doch das Falten und Einschneiden einer kontinuierlichen Oberfläche, durch die sich die Konturen der eigentlichen Gebäudeteile erst abzeichnen, zum Prinzip der Dachlandschaft: Der Boden wird zur Wand, Treppen und Rampen verschmelzen in der Oberfläche. Nicht nur der Entwurf des Tragwerks selbst, sondern auch die – durch die Erdbebengefahr – erhöhten Ansprüche an die Struktur forderten einige Monate intensiver Arbeit aller beteiligten Büros.

Schließlich wurde eine simple Idee zum Grundprinzip des Tragwerks. Die Anordnung der Haupt- und Nebenträger greift das statische Prinzip der Kuppelform auf, um die Spannweiten von 16 Metern möglichst elegant zu überbrücken und gleichzeitig die höheren Dachlasten aufzunehmen. Dennoch musste man sich von einigen Ideen, wie etwa dem Gedanken, das ganze Dach begehbar zu machen oder gar eine Joggingbahn über die Mall laufen zu lassen, verabschieden. Letztlich wird das ganze Dach zwar eine durchgehende Graslandschaft, die begehbare Fläche aber auf 1000 Quadratmeter beschränkt. Der Rest wird mit einem Dünengras bepflanzt, das nicht gemäht wird und wild in die Höhe sprießt. Wie ein wogendes Feld erscheint das Dach, wenn der Wind über das Gebäude weht. Das Gründach ist jedoch weit mehr als ein urbanes Gestaltungselement. Es erfüllt wichtige Funktionen, die gut sind für das Gebäudeklima: So hält es den Regen zurück, bindet Staub- und Luftschadstoffe und schirmt Hitze wie Kälte ab.

Da der Grünlayer relativ dünn war und teilweise auf sehr steile Gefälle oder gar unzugängliche Flächen aufgebracht werden musste, war auch hier wieder das gesamte Know-how der beteiligten Firmen und Planer gefordert. Das Dach wird übrigens automatisch bewässert, was vor allem am Anfang den Anwuchs der jungen Pflanzen sehr vereinfachte.

CHALLENGES OF THE ARCHITECTURE Design is one thing, but project implementation is another. Not everything that architects design in three-dimensional programmes can be realized unproblematically – above all, when it is a case of such exceptional and unconventional architecture as that of FOA. One of the greatest challenges of the design was the roof construction.

Structural engineers prefer a uniform construction, because it enables easier calculations relating to static equilibrium. But the design of 'Meydan' is anything but uniform, for the folding and intersecting of a continuous surface, through which the contours of the actual parts of the building appear, is part of the principle of the roof landscape: The floor becomes a wall, stairs and ramps merge into the surface. Not only the design of the load-bearing structure itself, but also the structural criteria (increased by the risk of earthquakes) demanded some months of intensive work on the part of all the firms involved.

Finally, a simple idea became the basic principle of the load-bearing structure. The arrangement of the main and subsidiary supports takes up the engineering principle of the cupola form, in order to bridge as elegantly as possible the span of 16 metres and at the same time take up the greater load of the roof. However, some ideas had to be abandoned, such as that of making the whole roof accessible or even installing a jogging track above the mall. In the final design, the entire roof becomes a totally grassed landscape, but the accessible area is restricted to 1,000 square metres. The rest is planted with a marram grass that is not cut, but shoots wildly up into the air. When the wind blows over the building, the roof looks like a waving field. The green roof, however, is far more than an urban design element. It fulfils important functions that are beneficial for the building's climate: it keeps off the rain, lays the dust and atmospheric pollutants and protects from both heat and cold.

Since the green layer was relatively thin and had to be laid partly on very steep inclines or even inaccessible surfaces, here too the overall expertise of the participating firms and planners was required. The roof incidentally was automatically watered, which, above all at the start, greatly facilitated the growth of the young plants.

Grundprinzip des Tragwerks für die Dachlandschaft: Die Anordnung der Haupt- und Nebenträger greift das statische Prinzip der Kuppelform auf, um Spannweiten von 16 Metern überbrücken und höhere Dachlasten aufnehmen zu können. Basic principle of the supporting structure of the roof complex: the composition of main and secondary trusses has been taken from the structural system of the dome shape in order to span widths of 16 metres and to bear larger loads.

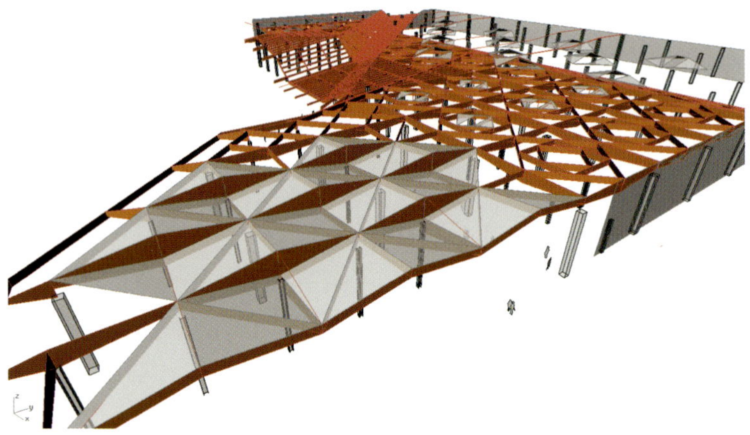

naturalbond
Aluminium Composite Panel

FASSADE Eine erodierte Landschaft – so die Grundidee des Entwurfs, die sich vor allem in der Begrünung des Dachs widerspiegelt. Doch auch die Außenfassaden sollten dieses Bild verstärken. Daher entschieden sich die Architekten bei der Wahl des Materials für Terrakotta, das dem Rotton der Erde in Ümraniye ähnelt. Das Prinzip weicht jedoch von herkömmlichen orthogonal gerasterten Fassaden ab. Inspiriert von den Außenwänden in der islamischen Architektur, sind circa 40 Prozent der verwendeten Platten perforiert und mit den geschlossenen Platten im Verband montiert. Dadurch entsteht eine kontinuierliche Oberfläche, die nur dort von perforierten Kacheln unterbrochen wird, wo Fluchtwege, Andienungsgänge oder Maschinenräume angeordnet sind.

Dieses Prinzip fand auch beim Kinogebäude Anwendung, das dadurch eine ganz eigene Ausstrahlung erhält: Durch den Wechsel von verschiedenen Raumtiefen hinter der Terrakottahaut wird die Massivität der Körper aufgeweicht. Dieser Effekt tritt besonders deutlich in den Abendstunden hervor, wenn die Baukörper von innen heraus beleuchtet werden – und sich das Gebäude in einem Lichtraster auflöst.

Während die Keramikfassaden die Außenseiten des Gebäudekomplexes begrenzen, wurden die inneren Wände, die den Platz umgeben, soweit wie möglich aufgelöst. Keine Konstruktion sollte die Kontinuität der Glashaut unterbrechen. Durch die Anwendung des Structural-Glazing-Prinzips ist die Trennung zwischen Shops und Platz auf eine zwei Zentimeter dünne Glashaut reduziert. Die verwendeten Formate der Glasscheiben gehen an die Grenzen des technisch Machbaren: Zwei mal vier Meter messen die größten Scheiben, bei einem Gewicht von rund 500 Kilogramm pro Stück.

Das Herzstück des gesamten Komplexes, der Platz, wurde ebenfalls in Anlehnung an die rötliche Erde in terrakottafarbenen Klinkern ausgeführt. Eine Reihe von Studien war notwendig, bis das optimale Muster gefunden wurde. Dieses nimmt die Grundrisslinien der Glasfassaden auf und wird dann konzentrisch zur Platzmitte geführt. Aufgelockert wird das Rot durch eine simple Reihung von helleren Steinen. Gewählt wurde ein vergleichsweise kleines Klinkerformat. Wie ein feinmaschig gewebtes Tuch wirkt die Oberfläche des Platzes dadurch.

Mit dem Klinker auf dem Platz verhält es sich übrigens ebenso wie mit dem Grün auf dem Dach: Ohne Unterbrechung fließt der Belag über den gesamten Komplex, wird zur Wand, Treppenanlage oder Rampe, taucht in die Tiefgarage ab oder fließt auf das Dach.

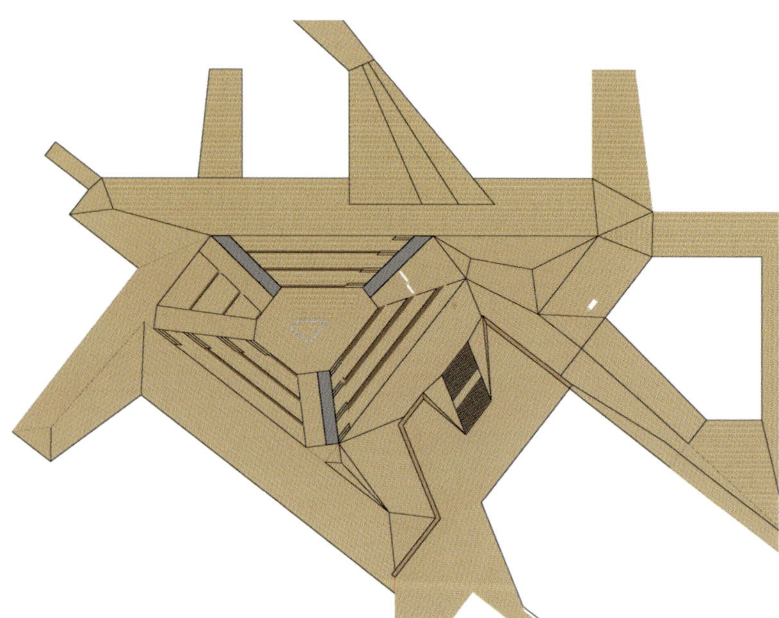

Ähnelt dem Rotton der Erde: Terrakotta wurde als Material für die Außenfassaden und die Platzgestaltung gewählt.
Similar to the earth's red colour: terracotta was the material chosen for the external facade and the square.

 An eroded landscape – that was the basic idea of the design, which above all is reflected in the planting of the roof. But the outer façades too were intended to support this picture. For this reason the architects, when choosing the material, decided in favour of terracotta, whose colour resembles that of the red soil at Ümraniye. The principle however diverges from the traditional orthogonally screened façades. Inspired by the outer walls of Islamic architecture, about forty of the panels used were perforated and mounted together with the closed panels. This creates a continuous surface which is interrupted by perforated tiles only where escape routes, delivery passages or machine-rooms are positioned.

This principle was also used in the cinema building, which thus acquires a charisma all of its own. Through the alternation of different dimensions of space behind the terracotta skin, the massivity of the structures is softened. This effect is seen particularly clearly in the evening hours, when the structures are lit from within, and the building seems to dissolve into a pattern of light.

While the ceramic façades border the outer sides of the building complex, the interior walls that surround the square were loosened up as much as possible. No structure would be allowed to break up the continuity of the glass skin. The use of the structural glazing principle reduces the separation between shops and square to a two-centimetre-thick glass skin. The formats used for the glass panels go to the limits of what is technically possible: The largest panels measure two by four metres, and weigh around 500 kilograms each.

The centrepiece of the whole complex, the square, was also executed in terracotta clinker brick, in allusion to the local reddish soil. A series of studies had to be conducted before the optimal pattern was found. This picks up the ground plan lines of the glass façades and is then taken concentrically to the centre of the square. The red colour is relieved by a simple sequence of light-coloured stones. A comparatively small clinker format was chosen. As a result the surface of the square looks like a finely woven cloth.

The clinker brick on the square is used in the same way as the greenery on the roof: The covering flows uninterrupted across the entire complex, becoming a wall, staircase or ramp, dips down into the underground car park and flows over the roof.

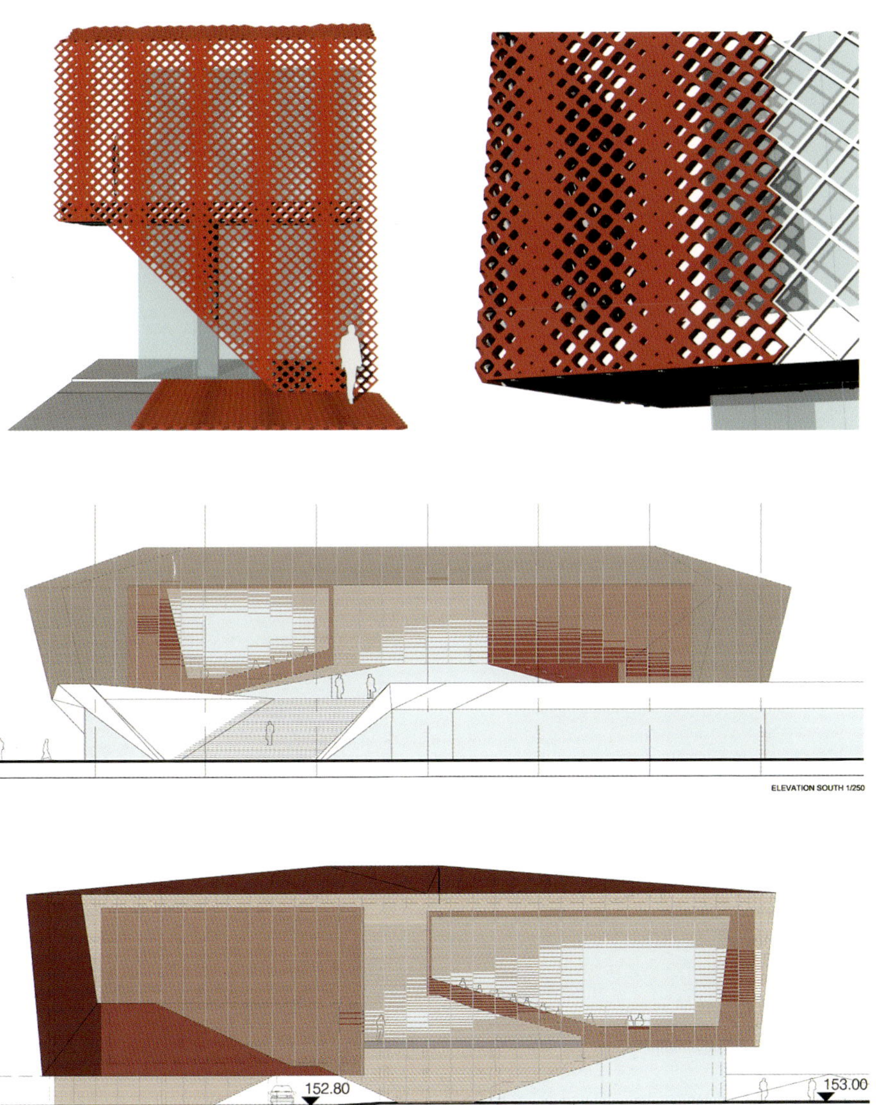

Perforierte Fassade am Kinokomplex: Durch den Wechsel
der verschiedenen Raumtiefen wird die Massivität des
Körpers aufgeweicht.
Perforated façade of the cinema complex: the alteration of
varying spatial depth breaks up the solidity of the volume.

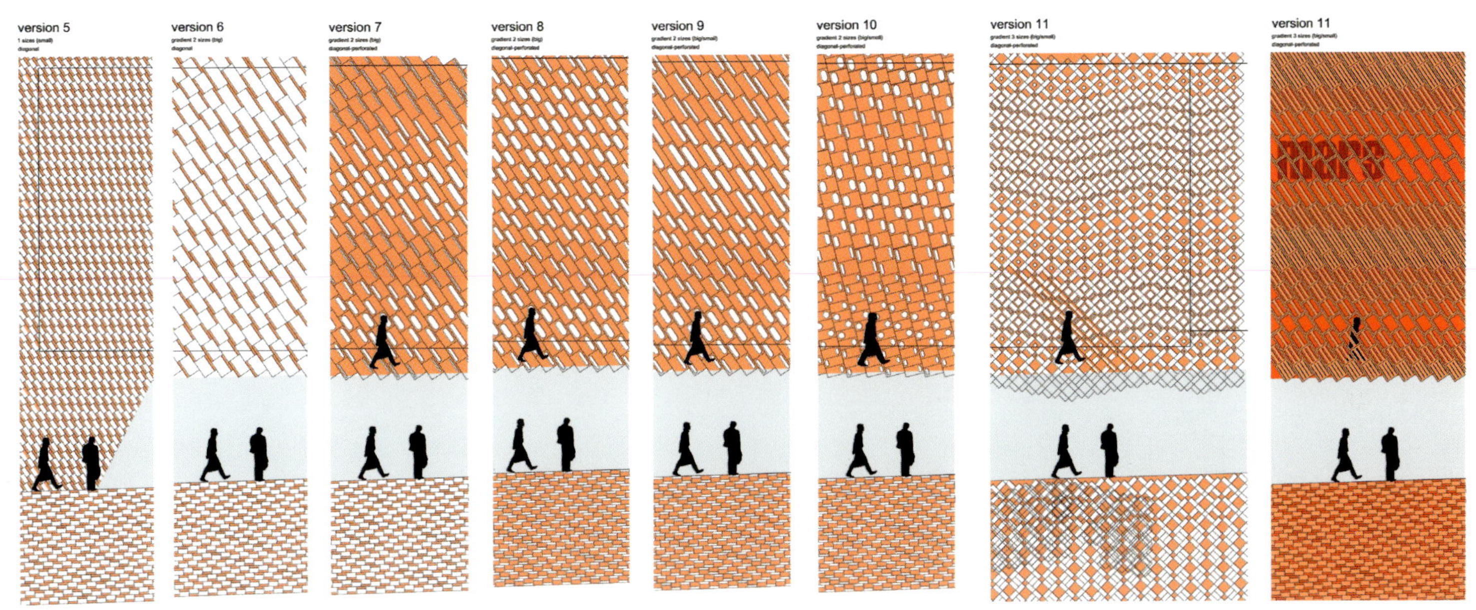

version 5
1 sizes (small)
diagonal
version 6
gradient 2 sizes (big)
diagonal
version 7
gradient 2 sizes (big)
diagonal-perforated
version 8
gradient 2 sizes (big)
diagonal-perforated
version 9
gradient 2 sizes (big/small)
diagonal-perforated
version 10
gradient 2 sizes (big/small)
diagonal-perforated
version 11
gradient 3 sizes (big/small)
diagonal-perforated
version 11
gradient 3 sizes (big/small)
diagonal-perforated
floor tiles
version 9 tiles
version 10 tiles
version 11 tiles

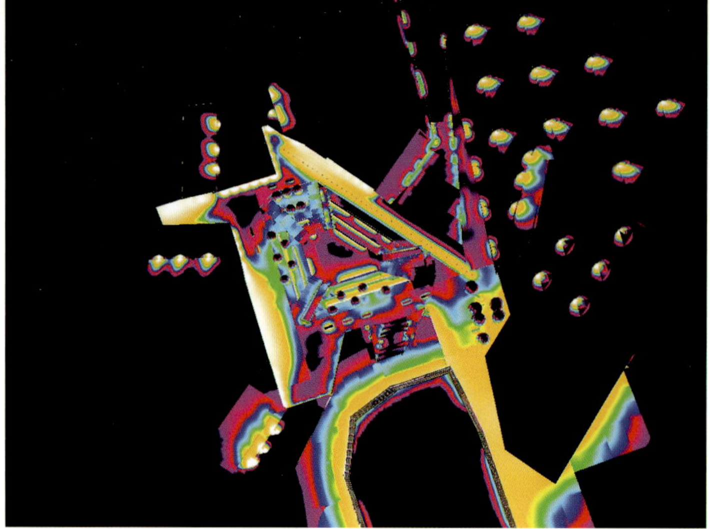

Architektur, die von innen strahlt: Lichtstudie für
den Komplex (Abbildung oben) und Umsetzung
(unten)
Architecture which shines from within: light
studies of the complex (above) and the finished
product (below)

LICHT   Schon während des Workshops war ein Lichtdesigner anwesend, verfolgte die verschiedenen Ansätze der Büros und gab Informationen über das Verhalten von natürlichem und künstlichem Licht. Im Zuge der Ausarbeitung mit FOA kristallisierte sich schnell der Wunsch heraus, dass die einzelnen Gebäude nicht inszeniert, also beleuchtet werden sollten, sondern die Architektur selbst strahlen sollte. Daher wurde möglichst mit indirektem Licht gearbeitet; der Platz und die Dachflächen bekamen Leuchtstelen, die dem Gebäude zu entwachsen scheinen. Die Anordnung erfolgte strikt nach der benötigten Position, um den Platz optimal auszuleuchten.

Um die Transparenz der Keramikfassaden hervorzuheben, wurden an der Innenseite der Fassaden RGB-Leuchten angebracht, die das Innere des Komplexes in jeder gewünschten Farbe beleuchten können. Die Lichtübergänge sind fließend und organisch. Fast scheint es, als würde das Gebäude atmen.

Auch die Beleuchtung der Innenräume ist bemerkenswert, wurde sie doch in die Gebäudestruktur integriert. So scheint zum Beispiel die ansonsten massiv wirkende Betondecke in der Tiefgarage aus sich heraus zu leuchten.

LIGHT   As early as the workshop stage a light designer was present, following the firms' various approaches and supplying information on the behaviour of natural and artificial light. In the course of the development of FOA's designs, the wish very quickly crystallized for the individual buildings not to be 'staged', that is, lit, but that the architecture itself should give out light. As far as possible, therefore, the architects worked with indirect light; The square and the roof surfaces were given light steles which seemed to grow out of the building. The arrangement was carried out strictly according to the position necessary to produce optimal illumination of the square.

To bring out the transparency of the ceramic façades, RGB lighting was installed on the inside of the façades, which could light the interior of the complex in any desired colour. The light transitions are flowing and organic. It almost seems as though the building is breathing.

The lighting of the interior spaces is also remarkable, since it has been integrated into the structure of the building. For example, the concrete ceiling in the underground car park, which would otherwise appear massive, seems to generate its own light.

DAS FERTIGE PROJEKT
THE COMPLETED PROJECT

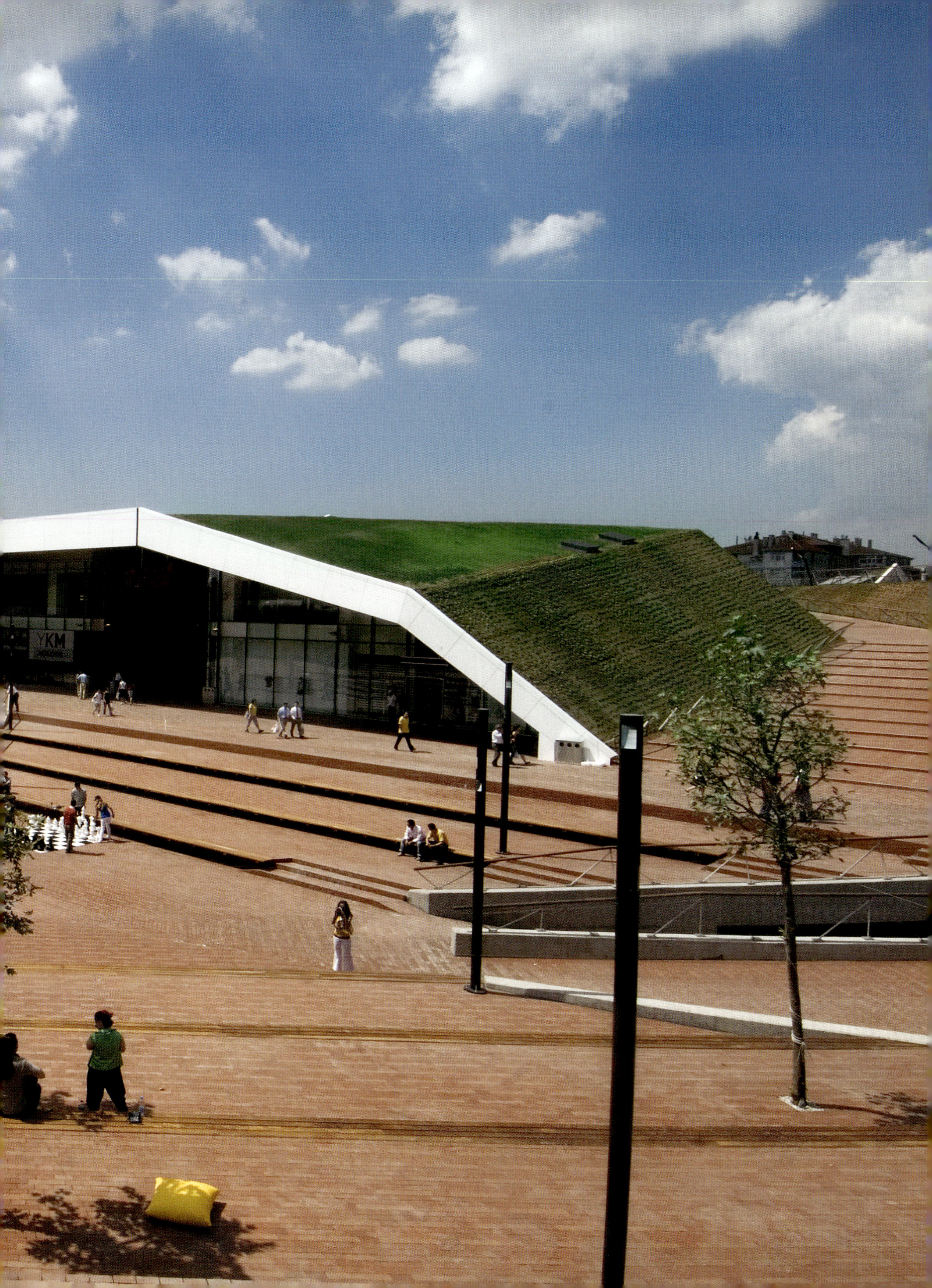
YKM

real,-
Media Markt
YKM
cinebonus
IKEA
YENI!
YENI!

Die Entwurfsvarianten zeigen Platzmodellierungen.
Design variations showing different shapings of the
square.

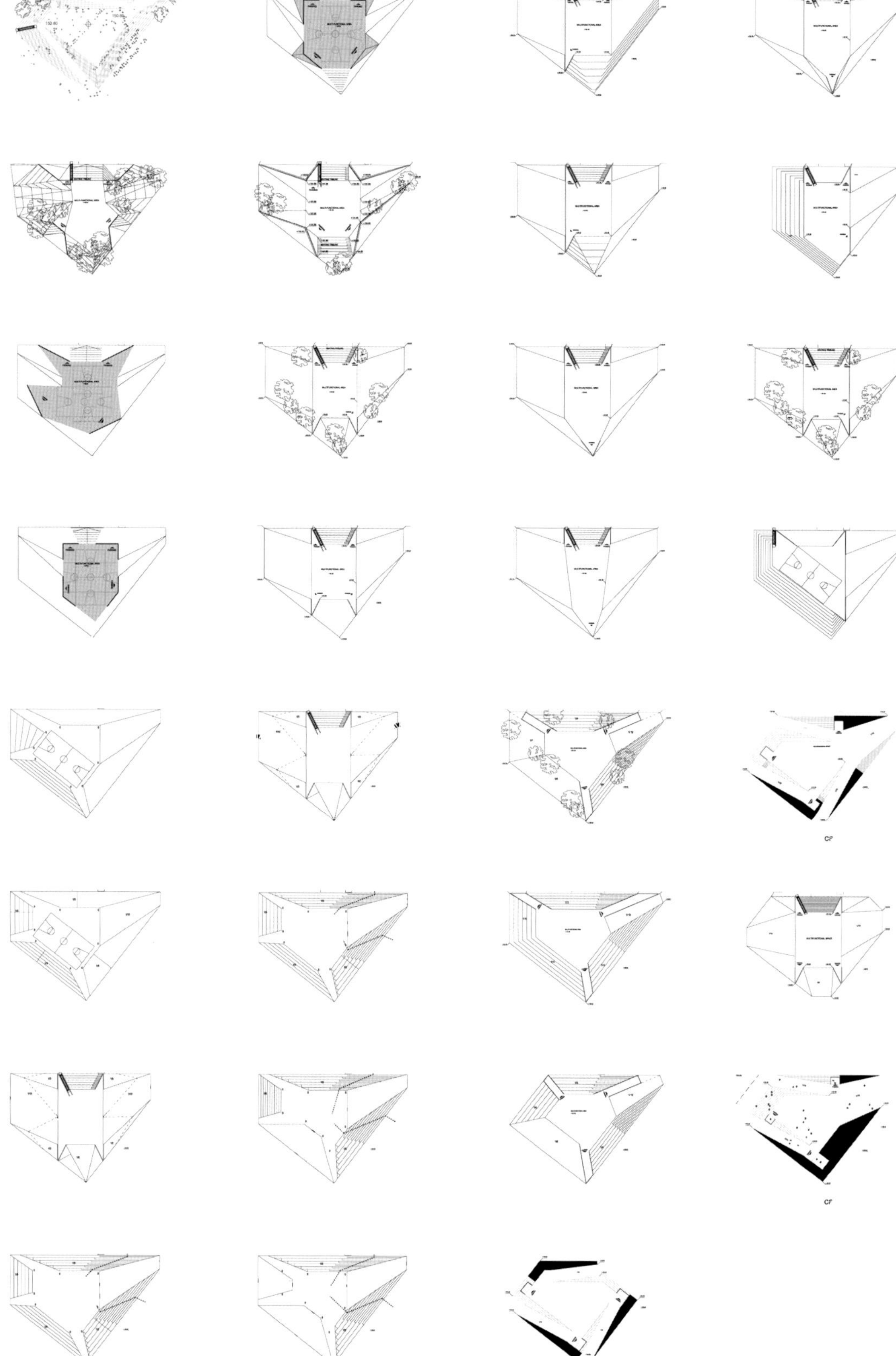

MERAL YAPI A.Ş.

MANGO
CHEVIGNON
real

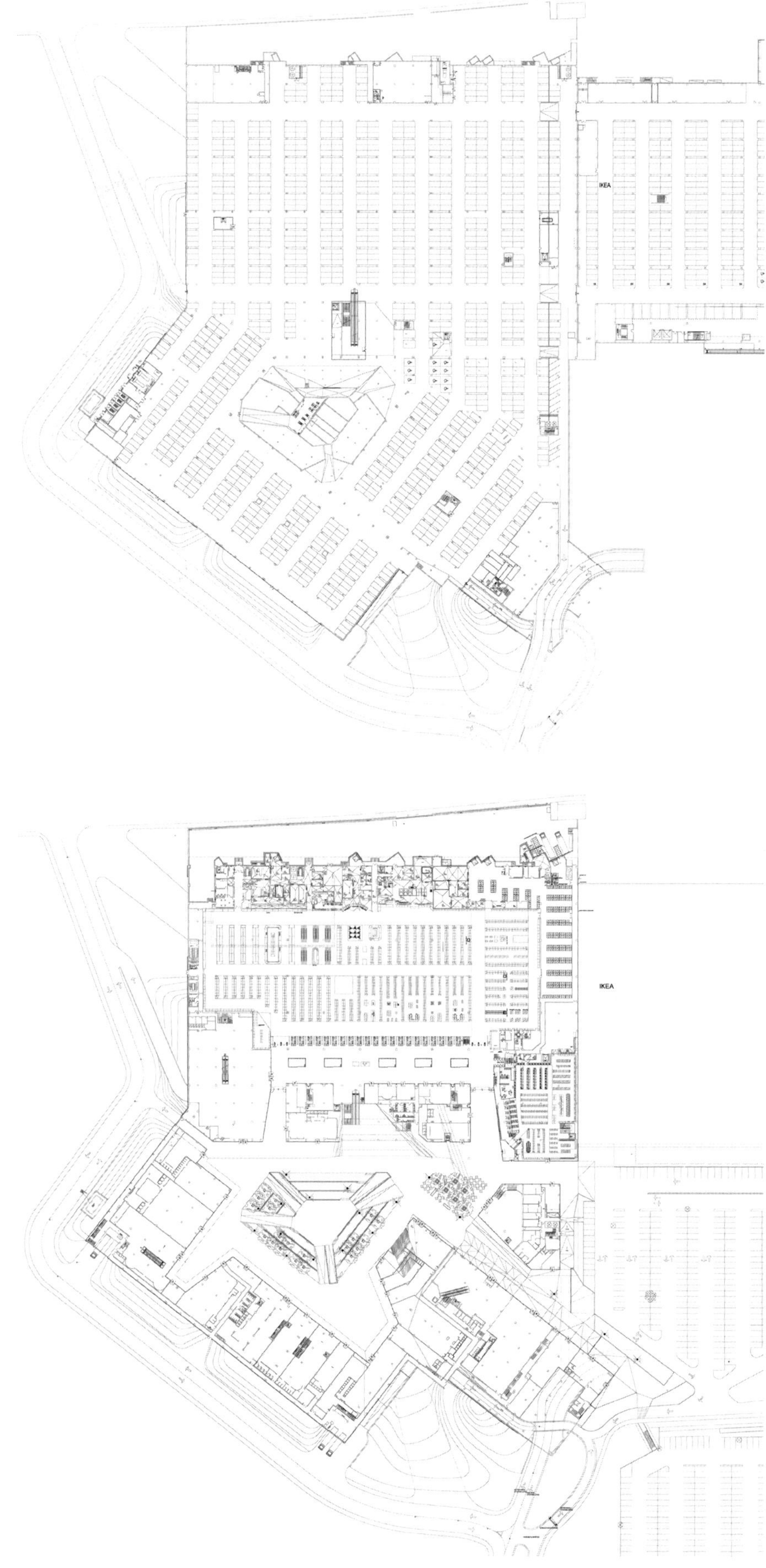
IKEA
IKEA

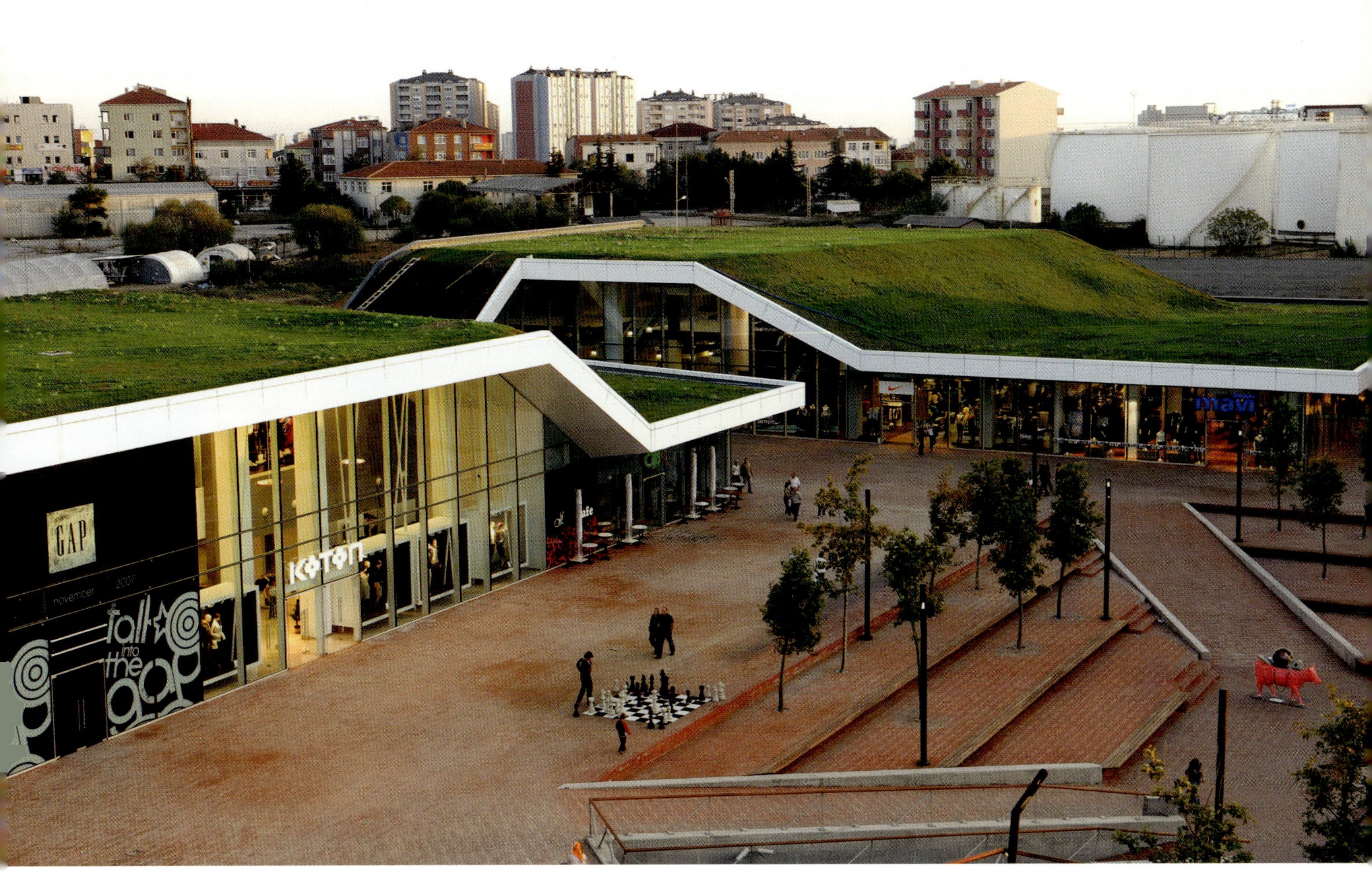

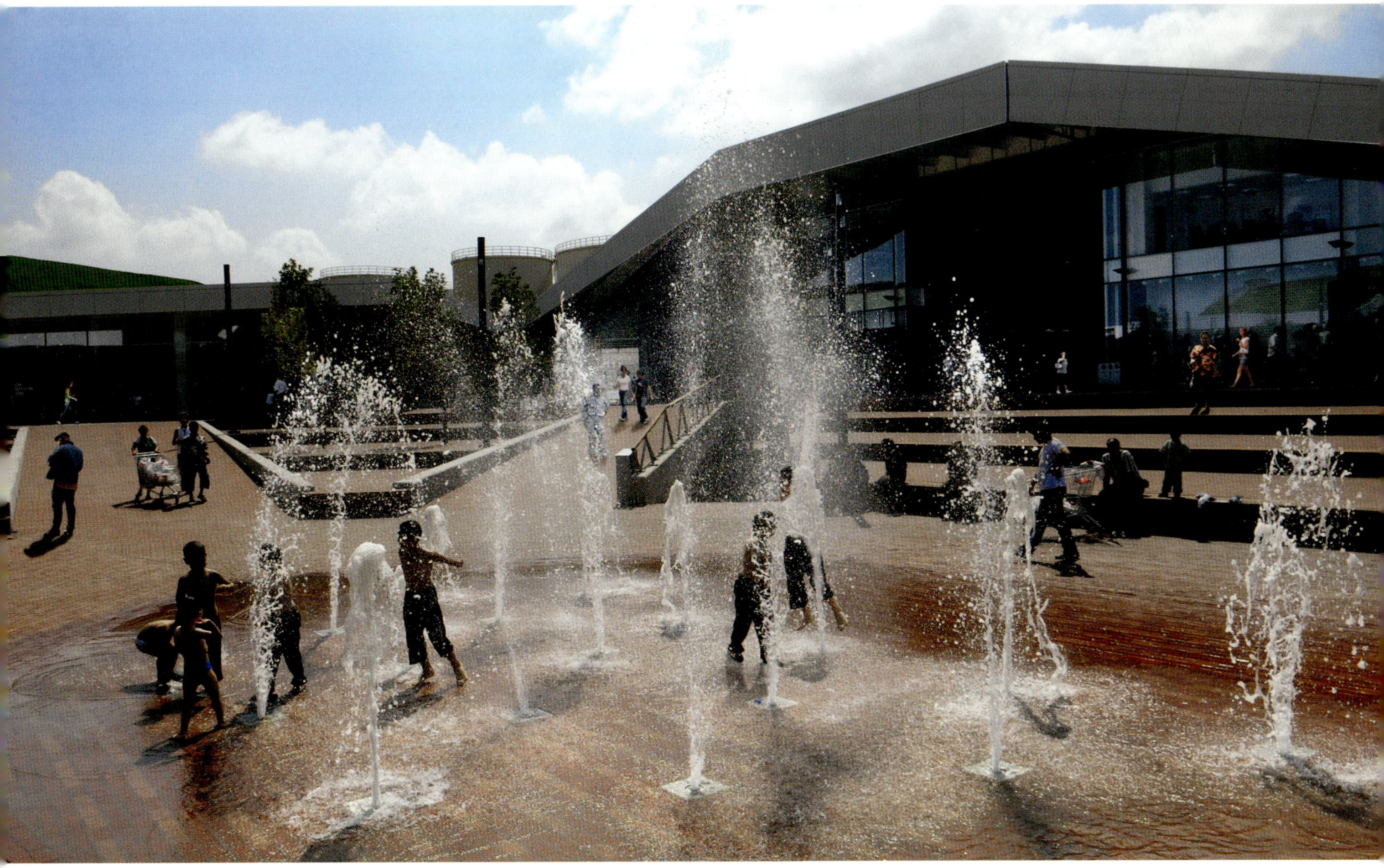

Media Markt
LCD · BILGISAYAR · HIFI · DVD/CD · TELEKOM · FOTO · EV ALETLERI
NGTON
CALL DUTY 4
MODERN WARFARE
SOLINLE
Panasonic
TITANIC
SABA
iş

Popeyes
CHICKEN & BISCUITS
Ramiz

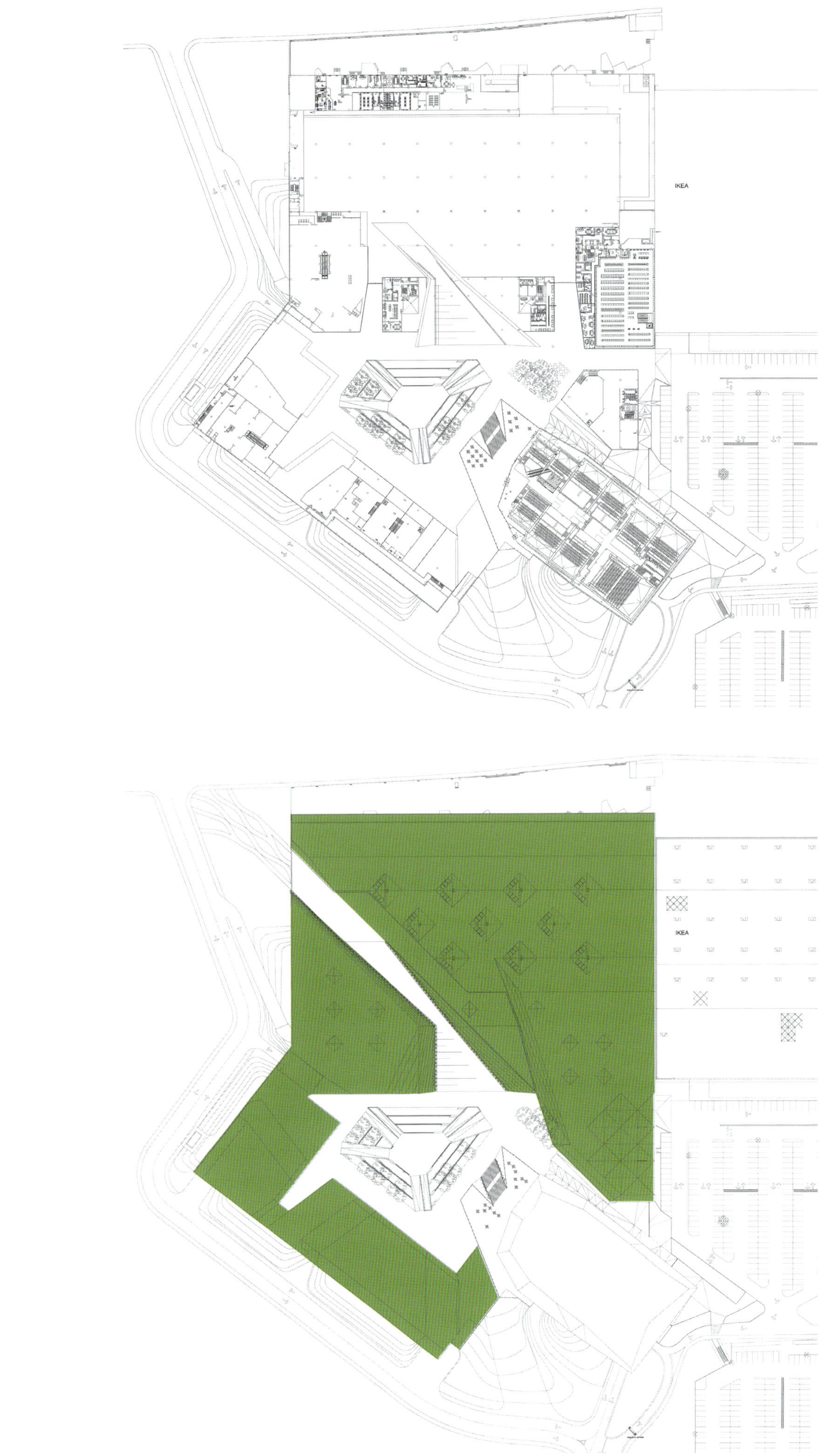

IKEA
IKEA

MUDO COLLECTION

Media Markt
Media Markt

YKM

Ein Sonntag in Meydan. Straßenmusikanten haben sich im Schatten postiert, ihre Musik tönt über den Platz, mischt sich mit dem heiteren Geplauder der Leute auf den Stufen und dem schnarrenden Geräusch der Skateboards, die von ein paar Jungs kunstvoll über Rampen und Treppen gesteuert werden. Die Tische vor den Cafés sind gut besetzt. Eine junge Frau zeigt ihrer Freundin, was sie sich kurz zuvor gekauft hat. Eine Mutter ruft den Nachwuchs zusammen, der gerade mit großzügig gefüllten Eistüten über den Platz schlendert. Und ein paar Tische weiter haben ein paar Teenager ihre Laptops aufgeklappt und betrachten kichernd Fotos aus den letzten Ferien. Eine Ebene darüber, auf dem Dach des Gebäudes, zeigt sich ein sehr typisches Bild für Istanbul, in dem jede freie Rasenfläche – sei sie im Park oder am Straßenrand – sofort von Menschen als Ruheplatz genutzt wird: Ein paar Familien sitzen auf Decken und zelebrieren ihr Picknick. Dabei schweift ihr Blick immer wieder über das Leben auf dem Platz – sowie die Dächer von Istanbul.

Eine Oase, so hat unter anderem die türkische Zeitung *Hürriyet* den neuen Platz in Ümraniye genannt. Und Umwelt- und Forstminister Osman Pepe staunte darüber, dass die bebaute Fläche nun grüner sei als vorher. „Normalerweise, und das ist ein großes Problem aller Städte, verschwinden Grünflächen durch die Bebauung", erklärte er während der Eröffnung des ersten Teilstücks des Gebäudekomplexes im August und stellte erfreut fest, dass es bei Meydan andersherum gewesen sei.

Doch noch mehr als der städtebauliche Effekt des neuen Zentrums für Ümraniye machte dessen Umweltfreundlichkeit Schlagzeilen. „Das erste Shoppingcenter der Welt, das heizt und kühlt, ohne fossile Brennstoffe zu nutzen", titelte etwa die Zeitung *Radical*. Die Tageszeitung *Sabah* listete fasziniert die Vorteile der Geothermieanlage auf und erklärt, wie dadurch rund 1,3 Millionen Kilowattstunden Primärenergie und 350 Tonnen umweltschädlicher CO_2-Emissionen pro Jahr eingespart werden. „Ein Beitrag für die Menschen und die Umwelt" ist Meydan für Minister Pepe, „ein Ausdruck der Liebe und des Respekts vor der Natur".

Ein weiterer Begriff fand sich häufig in den ersten Presseberichten über Meydan: Mit einem Basar nach altem osmanischen Vorbild wird das Center in Verbindung gebracht. Der Grund für die Assoziation ist die thematische Zusammenfassung der diversen Geschäfte in den einzelnen Themenwelten. „Inspiriert von alten Basaren bauten wir verschiedene Gassen für verschiedene Produktthemen", wird Prof. Michael Cesarz von METRO Group Asset Management in der Tageszeitung *Cumhuriyet* zitiert. Und tatsächlich beschreibt das türkische Wort „Meydan" nicht einfach nur einen ganz normalen Platz, sondern einen Ort, der sehr viel lebendiger und farbenfroher ist, einen öffentlichen Platz – oder: einen Basar.

Sunday in Meydan. Street musicians have positioned themselves in the shade; their music rings out through the square, mingling with the cheerful chatter of the people on the steps and the rasping sound of the skateboards being skilfully steered by a few boys over ramps and steps. The tables outside the cafés are busy. A young mother is showing her friend what she has just been buying. A mother calls to her offspring, who are strolling across the square with generously filled ice-cream cones. A few tables away, a couple of teenagers have opened their laptops and are giggling over their recent holiday photos. One level higher, on the roof of the building, shows a very typical view of Istanbul, where every free area of lawn – whether in the park or on the roadside – is immediately used by people as a resting place; a couple of families are sitting on blankets, enjoying a picnic, while their gaze constantly wanders over the life in the square – and also over the roofs of Istanbul.   An oasis – that is what the new square in Ümraniye has been called by the Turkish newspaper Hürriyet, among others. The Minister for the Environment and Forestry, Osman Pepe, expressed surprise that the built-up area was now greener than before. "Normally, and this is a great problem in all cities, green spaces disappear as a result of development," he commented during the opening of the first part of the building complex in August, noting with gratification that with Meydan it had been the other way around.

But even more than its effect on urban planning, the new centre in Ümraniye made the headlines because of its environmental friendliness. "The first shopping centre in the world to heat and cool without using fossil fuels," was a typical headline in the newspaper Radical. The daily paper Sabah listed, with fascination, the advantages of the geothermal system and explained how it was saving some 1.3 million kilowatt/hours of primary energy and 350 tonnes of environmentally harmful CO_2 emissions per year. Minister Pepe calls Meydan "a contribution to mankind and the environment, an expression of love and respect for nature."

Another concept was repeatedly mentioned in the first press reports on Meydan: The centre has been compared to the old Ottoman model of the bazaar. The reason for this association is the thematic grouping of the various shops into separate themed areas. "Inspired by the old bazaars, we built different streets for different products," Prof. Michael Cesarz of METRO Group Asset Management is quoted as saying in the daily newspaper Cumhuriyet. And in fact the Turkish word meydan describes not simply a normal square, but a place that is much more lively and colourful, a public square – or a bazaar.

Ein Shopping Square ist Meydan, keine klassische Shopping Mall, kein klassisches Shoppingcenter. Es ist eine Handelsimmobilie, die mehr sein will als das – und es auch schafft: die einem neuen Stadtteil ein soziales Zentrum gibt, wo sich die Menschen treffen, entspannen und etwas erleben können. Die Idee ist dieselbe wie die von Victor Gruen, dem Erfinder der Shoppingcenter. Auch er wollte einst einen öffentlichen Raum schaffen, der soziale Funktionen erfüllt und nicht nur zum Kaufen animiert. Doch die Weiterentwicklung der Malls entfernte sich sehr schnell von diesem Ansatz. Jetzt knüpfen METRO Group Asset Management und FOA wieder daran an. Doch während sich Gruen von den Passagen des ausgehenden 19. Jahrhunderts inspirieren ließ und er der Überzeugung war, dass öffentliche Räume am besten wetterfest funktionieren und eine Mall als Baukörper nicht Bezug nehmen muss auf die umliegende Bebauung, hat man nun den Mut, sich zu öffnen: gegenüber dem Himmel wie auch gegenüber dem Umfeld. Nicht die Passagen, sondern der klassische Marktplatz inspirierte die Architekten bei ihrem Entwurf. „Wir waren experimentierfreudig und wollten in Ümraniye etwas Neues ausprobieren, was gleichzeitig auch Antworten gibt auf die städtebaulichen Entwicklungen vor Ort", erklärt METRO AG-Vorstand Zygmunt Mierdorf, „entstanden ist ein Marktplatz der Moderne, der mit Sicherheit einen prägenden Impuls für die Handelsarchitektur der kommenden Generationen geben kann."

Es wird Abend in Ümraniye, die Sonne verschwindet langsam hinter dem Häusermeer. Die ersten Familien packen ihre Picknickkörbe, während sich auf den Stufen des Platzes immer mehr Jugendliche versammeln. Sie wollen ins Kino; einige warten auf weitere Freunde, andere darauf, dass es Zeit wird, in das Gebäude hineinzugehen. Die Straßenmusiker von heute Morgen sind nicht mehr da, andere sind gekommen. Sie spielen türkischen Pop, Rhythmen, bei denen man nicht gern sitzen mag. Ein paar Männer machen den Anfang: Sie bilden einen Kreis, fassen sich an den Händen und tanzen singend zur Musik. Das Kino dahinter leuchtet derweil in immer wechselnden Farben, taucht das Geschehen in jeweils andere Stimmungen und mimt den virtuosen Beleuchter für das Fest auf dem Platz.

Meydan is a shopping square, not a classic shopping mall, not a classic shopping centre. It is a commercial property that wants to be more than that – and succeeds: one which provides a social centre for a new urban district, where people can meet, relax and enjoy new experiences. The idea is the same as that of Victor Gruen, the inventor of the shopping centre. He too wanted to create a public space that would fulfil social functions and not only encourage people to buy. But the further development of the malls very soon moved away from this approach. Now METRO Group Asset Management and FOA are returning to it. But while Gruen was inspired by the arcades of the late nineteenth century and was convinced that public spaces function best when protected from the weather, and that a mall as a building need not take account of the surrounding development, the present developers have had the courage to open up – to the heavens as well as to the neighbourhood. It was not the arcades but the classical market place that inspired the architects in their design. "We were keen to experiment, and wanted to try out something new in Ümraniye which would also provide answers to the urban developments in the area," explains METRO AG chairman Zygmunt Mierdorf, "and the result is a market place of the modern era, a prototype that can also be used in other rapidly-growing cities and will certainly give a definitive stimulus to commercial architecture for generations to come."   Evening is falling in Ümraniye; the sun disappears slowly behind the sea of houses. The first of the families start to pack up their picnic baskets, while more and more young people gather on the steps of the square. They are planning to go to the cinema, some expecting the arrival of more friends, others waiting for the right time to enter the building. The street musicians of the morning have left, and others have taken their place. They are playing Turkish pop music, rhythms which make it difficult to sit still. A few men make a start; they form a circle, join hands and dance, singing to the music. Behind them, meanwhile, the cinema glitters with ever-changing colours, bathing the dancers in alternating moods, like a skilled technician creating the lighting for a celebration on the square.

WANTED
DEAD OR ALIVE
THE "WILDERNESS TRAVELLER"
Wanted for the very FINEST AUTHENTIC rugged
wearing, yet comfortable as broke in saddle
REWARD OF $2500

FUN WHEEL
smart 500
smart 500

ÇOK YAKINDA...BURADAYIZ!
MUDO COLLECTION
fts
64
ŞEHİR...BİZİM!
www.fts64.com

real,-
YKM

Bauträger Property developer: **METRO Group Asset Management,**
                                                     Düsseldorf, Istanbul
Designer/Architekt Designer/architect: FOA Foreign Office Architects/England
Architekt Architect: TAM-Turgut Aalton Mimarlik
                                                     Etud Mimarlik
Elektroinstallationsentwurf Electrical designer: ÖNEREN Engineering
                                                     Cont.Ltd.Co.
Ingenieurtechnischer Entwurf Mechanical designer: ÇILINGIROĞLU
                                                     Mühendislik ve Müş.Limited Şirket
Infrastruktur-Entwurf Infrastructure designer: KOROGLU Muh.
Projektmanagement Project management: IMS, Mühendislik
                                                     Danışmanlık ve Ticaret Ltd. Şti./Yapi-İnşaat
Statik Structural engineering: Adams Kara Taylor, London
                                                     Balkar İnşaat Mühendisliği, Istanbul
Gebäudeklimakonzept Air-conditioning concept: IP 5, Stuttgart
Außenanlagen Outdoor facilities: GTL, Gnüchtel Triebswetter Landschaftsarchitekten
Lichtplanung Lighting design: Luxwelt
Bauzeit Construction period: Shopping Square Meydan:
                                                     März March 2006–September 2007
Grundstück Site: 127.822 m²
Gesamtfläche BGF Total Gross floor area: 70.000 m² (ohne Parkplätze without parking)
                                                     130.000 m² (mit Garagen with parking garages)
Bebaute Grundfläche Building footprint: 50.000 m²

IKEA: 30.500 m²
Real: 14.500 m²
Kino Cinema: 4500 m²
Weitere Geschäfte Further shops: 18.500 m²

Weitere Geschäfte/Einheiten Further shops/units: 51
Gründach Green roof: 29.200 m²
Klinkerfassade Clinker façade: 62.120 Stück pieces
Bodenklinker Floor clinker bricks: 700.000 Stück pieces
Glassfassade Glass façade: 6100 m²
Geothermie Geothermal system: 200 Erdwärmesonden mit 50–150 Meter
                                                       Tiefe; Leistung bis 1500 KWh;
                                                       CO_2-Einsparung: 320 Tonnen/Jahr
                                                       200 geothermal probes at depth of 50–150 metres;
                                                       output up to 1500 KWh;
                                                       CO_2 savings: 320 tons/year

Bau in zwei Phasen Two building phases

Phase I 2005: Ikea und Parkplatz
Phase I 2005: Ikea and parking

Grundstück Site: 61.213 m²
BGF Gross floor area: 30.588 m²
Bebaute Grundfläche Building footprint: 19.722 m²
1. OG 1. Floor: 10.866 m²

Phase II 2007: Shopping Square Meydan

Grundstück Site: 66.609 m²
BGF Gross floor area: 39.412 m²
Bebaute Grundfläche Building footprint: 30.278 m²
1. OG 1. floor: 9134 m²